The
SATAN
Syndrome

The SATAN *Syndrome*

Putting The
Power of Darkness
In Its Place

NIGEL WRIGHT

Academie Books Grand Rapids, Michigan
Zondervan Publishing House

THE SATAN SYNDROME
Copyright © 1990 by Nigel Wright

Previously published in Great Britain by Marshall Morgan and Scott as
THE FAIR FACE OF EVIL © 1989 by Nigel Wright. This edition published
by special arrangement with Marshall Pickering, London

ACADEMIE BOOKS is an imprint of Zondervan Publishing House,
1415 Lake Drive, S.E., Grand Rapids, Michigan 49506.

Library of Congress Cataloging in Publication Data

Wright, Nigel G.
    The satan syndrome : putting the power of darkness in its place /
Nigel G. Wright.
      p.   cm.
    Includes bibliographical references.
    ISBN 0-310-53191-8
    1. Devil. 2. Good and evil. 3. Powers (Christian theology)
I. Title.
BT981.W75   1990
235'.4–dc20
                                      90-35403
                                      CIP

Printed in the United States of America

90 91 92 93 94 95 / AK / 10 9 8 7 6 5 4 3 2 1

With love and gratitude to the members of

Ansdell Baptist Church
Blackpool Christian Fellowship
South Fylde Community Church
Emmaus Fellowship, Blackpool

who have known the fight and tasted the victory.

Contents

CHAPTER ONE

The Satan Syndrome

So, the devil is back in business again. Of course, he's never really been out of it but it does seem that both in the world and in the church we are inclined to approach the devil with new found respect. Some of the old certainties have become muted. The rationalism which came to expression in the eighteenth century Enlightenment had little room for the idea of demons. In reaction to the dominant influence of church theology which had been characteristic of previous generations the balance shifted from reliance upon the authority of traditions or of scripture towards an emphasis upon the rational capacity of man. The principle of doubt became significant in man's quest for knowledge. Thinkers were no longer convinced about the validity of metaphysical speculation. Mankind's proper concern was conceived to be the objective, empirical world about which reasonable and verifiable statements could be made. Blaming the devil for things that could not easily be explained came to be seen as superstition, and dangerous superstition at that. The scientific revolution that was under way encouraged people to believe that everything could be explained by reference to natural processes all of which would one day be explained. Where does the devil fit into this increasingly unmysterious world? Come to think of it, where does God fit in?

No-one in their right mind would want to put the clock back three hundred years. The scientific, intellectual and industrial revolutions which shape our modern world have brought immense benefits. We might think most obviously of the material benefits that have delivered so many in the Western world from want and drudgery and have brought marvellous new possibilities within the reach of ordinary people. By and large we live longer and we live better because of the Enlightenment revolution in our understanding of ourselves and of our environment.

But other benefits are not so immediately obvious to us. It is at least arguable that the Enlightenment effected a deliverance from superstition which has set subsequent generations free from neurotic and paranoid fears of some kind of cosmic plot. For some reason buried deep in human psychology, the human mind easily embraces conspiracy theories. The world is a far simpler place in which to live if we are able to identify the enemy and project all our fears and doubts on to him, it or her. If I can attribute the rot in my society to the subversive influence (say) of Communist infiltrators then I have some sort of framework for living in the world. If I am able to identify Soviet Russia as the 'focus of evil in the modern world', then it makes it easier to decide what I must do. If, as in Nazi Germany, the ills of society can be blamed upon the Jews, then life's complex decisions become much easier, since somebody else is to blame and not me. The human mind has a liking for such conspiracy theories and for many in pre-Enlightenment Europe belief in the devil amounted to a conspiracy theory writ large.

It has been estimated that between 1450 and 1700 one hundred thousand people may have perished in what has been called 'the great witch craze'.[1] This was a movement that had its roots in the Inquisition, the medieval tribunal which attempted to eradicate heresy and witchcraft by the use of torture and executions. The climate of opinion which developed held that a cosmic plot directed by Satan threatened all Christian society. In Catholic and Protestant territories alike 'millions were persecuted and tens of millions terrified and intimidated during one of the longest and strangest delusions in history'.[2] The disturbing point to note is that such a craze could only have developed in areas where people looked at the world from a Christian point of view. It was the Enlightenment that put an end to the witch craze. Its reasoned and scientific approach to life had no room for witchcraft. In the light of the facts it is difficult to regret this.

It is not therefore altogether surprising that for several hundred years Satan has experienced something of an eclipse in the consciousness of most Western people. According to Walter Wink, angels, demons and the devil have become the unmentionables of our society, the 'drunk uncle' that people would rather forget about. In ' "sophisticated" circles accounts of sexual exploits scarcely raise an eyebrow, but if you want to bring all talk to a halt in shocked embarrassment, every eye riveted on you, try mentioning angels, or demons, or the devil. You will quickly be appraised for signs of pathological violence and then quietly shunned'.[3] The devil has come to be seen in society and in the church as a piece of mythological baggage which belongs to a previous and outdated worldview.

With only sense, experience and reason to go on, and with no rational place for an evil first cause, enlightened people simply dropped the devil from consideration. With direct psychic experience no longer admissible as evidence of his reality, the devil was as good as dead.[4]

While among thinking people the devil was being re-interpreted as the external projection of mankind's own internal demons, the church also felt the force of the problem. The intellectual revolutions of the eighteenth century raised the question (one which is still with us), of how literally we are to understand the Bible. If we now no longer accept the biblical worldview of a three-storey universe, why should we continue to believe in the devil? So the devil became a candidate for demythologising. Rudolf Bultmann spoke, and speaks, for many when he wrote:

> No-one can use the electric light and the radio or the discoveries of modern medicine and at the same time believe in the New Testament world of spirits and miracles.[5]

Few theologians would argue that the New Testament references to the devil are meaningless, but the large majority would argue that they need to be reinterpreted for a scientific age. So it is that the 'demons' of the Gospels are to be understood as the primitive descriptions of afflictions now treated by physicians and psychiatrists, while the 'principalities and powers' of Paul's letters are said to correspond to the concerns of present day politicians and sociologists.[6] The clear implication is that the notion of the devil and of demons is no longer necessary in our world. The devil has outlived his usefulness. His services are no longer required.

Yet, dead though he may be, the devil refuses to lie down. This is evidenced by the fact that even in scientific, technological societies such as our own there is a resurgence of interest in the devil. This is evidenced in a number of ways.

1. The inadequacy of materialism

It seems to be the case that humankind is not satisfied with purely materialistic explanations of human existence. Human experience cannot be reduced to purely scientific categories and there have consistently been reactions against attempts to do this. The Enlightenment was followed by the Romantic movement, a revolt against purely rational explanations of life which took no account of the mysterious and mystical dimensions of human experience. Romanticism found great depths and heights in the beauties of nature, literature and music which were seen as testimonies to the supernatural capacities of human beings. A recent radio interview with the barrister and novelist John Mortimer, a man long known for his atheism, revealed a similar tendency. Mortimer spoke of his increasing interest in religion, of his recognition of the need for a mystical aspect to life and of the fact that he believed everything about Christianity except for the existence of God![7] Though there has been a decline in Christian faith in our own culture, it could not be said that there has necessarily been a decline in religion. Though less Christian, people are not necessarily less religious. It is simply that other forms of religious expression have moved into the space left unoccupied by Christianity. Many of these new forms of religion may be described as secular religions, or even as idolatry. But they testify to the fact that humankind is incurably religious or, as somebody has said: '*Homo sapiens* is *ipso facto homo religiosus*', human beings are intrinsically religious.[8]

The remarkable thing is that despite years of secularising influence there still arise in the human heart the desire and the need for a non-materialistic perspective on their lives. This may help to explain why it is that language about God and the devil continues to have currency in our own culture. Although people have difficulty with the thought of God or the devil, something about human experience finds expression in this way and cannot adequately be expressed in any other way. The use of the language (outdated though it may seem to many) thus 'allows us to reclaim, name and comprehend types of experience that materialism renders mute and inexpressible'.[9] The world is far more mysterious a place than the purely materialistic understanding of it would lead us to suppose and paradoxically it is the ongoing march of science which is increasingly confirming the basic human instinct which seeks for spiritual fulfilment.

2. The experience of the twentieth century

This is a further factor that explains the enduring usefulness of 'diabolical' language. It seems hard now to believe that the century opened with a sense of hope and optimism about the perfectibility and progress of mankind. The carnage of the Great War and the unspeakable blasphemies of the Nazi era and the Second World War have left us in a far more chastened mood. The events of the Third Reich are hard to describe in ordinary language. How can we account for the way in which one of the most advanced nations on earth became effectively demonised? Or what manner of forces could produce the indescribable horror of the holocaust? The events of that period continue to appal, fascinate and elude subsequent generations as we try to come to terms with the horrific magnitude of it all. To cite Emil Brunner:

A generation which has produced two world wars, and a totalitarian state with all its horrors, has very little cause to designate the Middle Ages as 'dark'. . . . On the contrary it is just because our generation has experienced such diabolical wickedness that many people have abandoned their former 'enlightened' objection to the existence of a 'power of darkness', and are now prepared to believe in Satan as represented in the Bible.[10]

In response to such experiences it is significant that theologians have begun to reflect again upon the nature of the demonic. In the face of actual experience it becomes increasingly necessary to bring the devil back from retirement and press him into service again.

The Second World War is only the tip of the iceberg. Increasingly while psychology has opened up the drives and impulses which unconsciously shape human beings, sociology has opened up the reality of suprapersonal forces which shape human societies. Mankind is not completely the master of its own fate but is held by a network of social, political, economic and cultural forces which make it what it is. When confronted with the apartheid system of South Africa, the divided communities of Northern Ireland, the deprived and exploited areas of the Third World, the impersonal capitalism of multinational companies, we search for language to describe the suprahuman powers which are at work and are pushed in the direction of the category of the demonic.

3. The growth of occultism

A little over twenty-five years ago a writer on the subject clearly envisaged that witchcraft would continue its rapid dying process in the face of 'the popular press, popular education, a national health scheme, and the American Way of Life'![11] Clearly, at that time there was little indication of the explosion in occult interest which has taken place since then. It is not my intention to chart this explosion since others have written more than enough on the subject already.[12] We simply need here to register the growth of interest in the paranormal that has taken place within recent decades and to attempt to gain a perspective on it. It may be helpful to distinguish four aspects of such interest.

(a) Scientific interest. Since human claims to be affected by an invisible world of reality which somehow interacts with the visible world are widespread and persistent, scientists have begun to regard this as an area of legitimate investigation. This enquiry is sometimes called 'parapsychology' and as a scientific discipline it has yet to gain the acceptance and respect of other disciplines. No doubt this non-acceptance is owing to the fact that parapsychology is unable to prove itself within the accepted canons of scientific research. 'Psi' (the hypothetical energy force which is under investigation) and the psychic phenomena it produces tend to be somewhat elusive. The result is that after nearly fifty years of research, parapsychology has little to show by way of assured results beyond the conclusion (based on experiments in statistical probability) that some forms of extrasensory perception seem possible.[13] Of course, the lack of assured results may itself be due to the fact that there is a dimension of reality at work here which is not subject to the ordinary methods of the material or behavioural sciences. As Christians would want to claim the same for the experience of knowing God, it may well be the case that other aspects of human experience cannot be analysed by science in its current state of understanding. At any rate, with whatever degree of success, recent years have seen the attempt to take seriously that dimension of experience which we call the 'paranormal' which has served to give a degree of acceptability to the subject.

(b) Human interest. Whatever science may or may not be able to prove seems to make very little difference to the fact that large sections of the human race take it for granted that humans possess what are best described as 'psychic powers'. Much of what is called the occult is simply the attempt to explore the inner world of human consciousness. It is commonly accepted that the conscious mind represents only the tip of the iceberg as far as the human psyche is concerned. There are vast uncharted regions which belong to the individual subconscious and even, as C. G. Jung argued, the racial subconcious. This is a fact to which we will have occasion to refer at several points of this book. It is conceivable that in the subconscious regions there are potentialities and possibilities which would surprise the conscious mind and which give rise to unusual phenomena, perceptions, trance-like states, healing abilities, religious emotions and ecstatic conditions without the need for us to refer either to the devil or to God by way of direct explanation. They are simply testimonies to the fertile and productive nature of the subconscious mind.

It is significant that Michael Perry in the book *Deliverance*, produced by the Christian Exorcism Study Group, finds it possible to understand a whole range of psychic phenomena without recourse to the devil or demons. Poltergeists, for instance, are not to be seen as essentially evil or malevolent but rather as in the nature of projections into the environment of psychic energy resulting from stressful situations. The appropriate Christian response to such phenomena is ministry to the situation of conflict and the formal blessing of individuals rather than exorcism.[14] Similarly, ghosts need not be seen as invariably the product of evil forces so much as 'place memories', imprints left on the environment by repetitive and sometimes emotion-laden events in the past which are picked up in certain circumstances in the present by a receptive individual.[15] Spiritualism is not to be seen as necessarily occult activity so much as 'a cult based on a somewhat credulous approach to highly selective aspects of paranormal phenomena'.[16] This book by Perry is noteworthy for its judicious and balanced approach and also for two further characteristics. Despite the lack of scientific proof, Perry and the group he represents appear to accept paranormal phenomena as part of the totality of human experience which, although not scientifically susceptible to categorisation can nevertheless be reflected upon and described as real experiences. Secondly, the book attributes much paranormal activity neither directly to God nor to the devil but to the human psyche. This is not to say that such activity is to be encouraged or approved of but it is to say that there is no need to see the devil in everything that may escape immediate comprehension and which does not fit into a Christian framework.

(c) Religious interest. Many Christians have not grasped the fact that occult activity does not necessarily imply an interest in Satan. The word 'occult' means 'hidden' and the self-perception of many who are modern-day occultists is that they are exploring a form of nature religion rather than making contact with the devil. Hence witchcraft sees itself as a revival of ancient paganism and of hidden knowledge about the nature and workings of the world. The powers of nature are used by witches, in this understanding, for both good and evil purposes.[17] For occultists therefore the motivation is an essentially religious one; witchcraft is a way of tapping into and being at one with the forces of nature. It is the search for a harmony and co-operation with the environment in which one is set and on which one depends. Christianity is seen as an intolerant religion which destroyed the ancient and indigenous religions and sought to impose a totalitarian ideology upon an otherwise easy-going and tolerant worship of nature.

(d) Satanic interest. Mixed in with the occult explosion is a further strand of interest which is specifically to do with the worship and service of Satan. Whereas witchcraft is essentially pre-Christian in its understanding of the supernatural world, Satanism is explicitly anti-Christian.[18] Satan is acknowledged as the ruler of the world and as Son of God. The church is hated and feared. Its ceremonies are parodied and despised. There is conscious antagonism towards Christians. Satanist groups are organised, disciplined and active in recruiting. They are a growing force.

The object of this description of the strands in the explosion of occult interest in recent years has been to indicate the variety of concerns which are at work within it. The power of darkness should not be regarded as equally or necessarily at work in every aspect of it and this is particularly to be stressed in regard to the scientific strand of interest.

4. The growth of the charismatic movement

A further reason for the resurgence of interest in the devil is the growth of the renewal movement in the church. This movement has led to a quickened awareness of the power of God and in its wake of that of the power of darkness. In charismatic groups spiritual warfare is a common emphasis. The earlier awareness of the ability of demons to afflict people has developed more recently into a concept of spiritual battle for the structures and wellbeing of society. These issues will be examined in their place. It is sufficient at the moment to stress that the reason for the writing of this book is precisely to reflect upon the kind of understanding of the power of darkness which will most help us in the task of renewing the life and mission of the church of God. It is essential to have a healthy understanding of this point precisely in order to keep our practice healthy.

There can be no doubt that the renewal of the deliverance ministry which is a growing aspect of charismatic renewal reflects the ministry of Jesus. The Son of God came into the world to destroy the works of the devil.[19] The ministry of Jesus was distinctively characterised by the fact that he set people free from the powers of darkness.[20] He also gave his disciples the authority to do the same and when they did so he declared that he saw Satan fall like lightning from heaven.[21] The ministry of deliverance should therefore be characteristic of God's people. But it would be foolish not to recognise that there are dangers. All warfare involves danger and in this sphere of ministry there are several which lie ready to hand.

(a) The pastoral danger. By this we mean that the potential to do harm to an individual who comes seeking for help in this area is considerable. By wrongly diagnosing the causes of an individual's condition and failing to discern the activity of evil spirits we may end up with a superficial diagnosis that does not reach the real cause of the problem. Equally, to diagnose demons where demons do not exist and engage in exorcism where what is needed is some other form of pastoral care and healing may lead us into aggressively invading a person's personality and causing serious damage. It is a worrying feature of much charismatic renewal that immature and irresponsible people attempt forms of ministry for which they are ill-informed and ill-equipped. The disciples of Jesus were hardly professionals but it could be said of them that they had been learning from the one who was more than able to cope in that particular situation and were far from being novices.

The practice in the more established churches of having properly recognised and trained individuals to work in this area along with a team of others including doctors and psychiatrists has much to commend it. Unfortunately, good sound practices of this kind are not so easy to establish in churches of a freer faith and order. Much concern in this area has arisen since the tragic case of the Barnsley exorcism trial in 1975 when a man murdered his wife after an all night exorcism. Having been told by his local vicar that he was possessed by forty demons, a group of charismatic Christians claimed to have exorcized many demons from the man but to have failed to remove the demon of murder.[22] This case should stand as a permanent reminder of the pastoral dangers which lurk in this area and should warn us about the need for carefully thought out practice and carefully trained workers in the deliverance field.

(b) The personal dangers. The personal dangers should not be underestimated. I refer at this point not so much to the dangers of temptation and of spiritual assault upon those who may be involved in ministry of this kind as to the possibilities of being deceived and caught up in something that may push us in directions in which we do not wish to go. Two examples from the recent past reinforce this point.

In 1980 a preacher and his friend tried to exorcise the 'spirit of Judas Iscariot' from a mentally unstable woman and unintentionally killed her by jumping up and down on her body. The judge at the trial acknowledged that they had acted with honourable motives.[23] Here the warning is not simply of the pastoral danger but of the personal danger of becoming involved with malevolent entities to such a degree that their nature inadvertently rubs off on the helper so that he or she becomes a little demonic themselves. In any kind of warfare the temptation is to become like the enemy. Here is a grave danger for those who work in this area.

A further example concerns the case of Derry Knight

13

who was found guilty at Maidstone Crown Court in 1986 of obtaining over £200,000 by false pretences from a group of Christians whom he persuaded that he was able to buy Satanic regalia and thereby destroy a Satanic organisation from within.[24] The danger present here is not so much that of becoming demonic in one's own behaviour as of being deceived. For those who are disposed to accept the reality of the power of darkness it then becomes possible to be drawn into a world which has its own form of credibility and consistency which cannot for the most part be verified. The possibilities of credulity are enormous. It becomes difficult to disentangle fact from fantasy. How do we distinguish between the real and sinister world of darkness and plain fantasy when Christians are by definition outside it? It is possible to lose a proper sense of judgement and by a credulous attitude give to the power of darkness more power than it actually possesses. This is where we come to the third danger area.

(c) The theological dangers. The theological dangers in this area are the main concern of this book. Others have written what needs to be said pastorally. The theological issue was eloquently stated by C. S. Lewis in the preface to *The Screwtape Letters* first published in 1942:

> There are two equal and opposite errors into which our race can fall about the devils. One is to disbelieve in their existence. The other is to believe, and to feel an excessive and unhealthy interest in them. They themselves are equally pleased by both errors and hail a materialist or a magician with the same delight.[25]

Lewis puts his finger on the issue. It is wrong to reject the existence of the powers of darkness but it is equally wrong to believe in them *in the wrong way*. The rest of this book may be taken as an exposition of this theme. It is precisely because the renewal movement is in danger of falling into the second of these errors that yet another book in this area may be considered necessary. My concern is how we may take the power of darkness seriously without taking it too seriously. It is the failure of Christians to get this right that concerns me as I write. The above quotation from C. S. Lewis is often used by Christian writers or speakers to warn Christians against an excessive interest in the power of darkness. Yet often I have come away from reading a book in this area or hearing a talk on the subject which far from filling me with joy has left me with the impression that the devil has been glorified. The point is not that Christians aim to do this but that something in our ways of thinking and speaking (in short in our theology) leaves us giving more respect to the devil than we should ever do.

At the beginning of *The Screwtape Letters* C. S. Lewis includes a quotation from Martin Luther which hits the nail on the head:

The best way to drive out the devil, if he will not yield to texts of Scripture, is to jeer and flout him, for he cannot bear scorn.

The intention of this book is not only to jeer at the devil and flout him but to offer ways of thinking and speaking about him (or it) that might deprive the devil of any respect from Christians and give the glory to God.

REFERENCES

1. Mircea Eliade (Ed) *The Encyclopaedia of Religion* Vol 5 (New York, 1987) p419.
2. ibid.
3. Walter Wink *Unmasking the Powers* (Philadelphia, 1986) p1.
4. Morton Kelsey 'The Mythology of Evil' in *Journal of Religion and Health* **13** (1974) p16 (cited by Wink *op cit* p9).
5. Rudolf Bultmann in H. W. Bartsch (Ed) *Kerygma and Myth* (London 1953) p5.
6. D. E. H. Whiteley *The Theology of St Paul* (Oxford, 1972) p19.
7. Kaleidoscope, Radio 4, 25 April 1985.
8. I owe this phrase to Dr Cyril Okeroche of Nigeria. It is an adaptation of the title of his article 'Homo africanus is ipso facto homo religiosus'.
9. Walter Wink *op cit* p7.
10. Emil Brunner *The Christian Doctrine of Creation and Redemption* (London, 1952) p135.
11. Pennethorne Hughes *Witchcraft* (Harmondsworth, 1965) p210.
12. See eg Michael Green *I Believe in Satan's Downfall* (London, 1975) pp112–126; John Richards *But Deliver Us From Evil* (London, 1974) pp12–90; Michael Perry *Deliverance* (London, 1987) pp44–70.
13. D. G. Brenner (Ed) *Encyclopaedia of Psychology* (Grand Rapids, 1985) p795.
14. Perry *op cit* pp13–26.
15. ibid pp27ff.
16. ibid p46.
17. ibid pp55–59.
18. ibid p62.
19. 1 Jn 3:8.
20. Lk 11:20.
21. Lk 10:17–19.
22. See John Allan *Dealing With Darkness* (Edinburgh, 1986) p1; Perry *op cit* p112; *The Times* 26 and 27 March 1975.
23. *The Times* 4 September 1980. See Perry *op cit* p112.
24. *The Times* 24 April 1986. Perry *op cit* p67.
25. C. S. Lewis *The Screwtape Letters* (London, 1942) p9.

CHAPTER TWO

Disbelieving in the Devil

Should Christians believe in the devil? The vast majority of Christians who believe in the final authority of the Bible will answer in the affirmative. There may be others, whether Christian or not, who find this objectionable. Yet those who do believe in the devil can at least argue that they are being consistent. If the Bible is to be believed in its witness concerning God, why should it not be equally believable in regard to the devil? And if belief in the devil is to be rejected, is not belief in God sure to follow in swift order?

In fact, whatever difficulties modern people may have with such a belief, all are bound to admit that the devil is taken with great seriousness in the New Testament. So much is this the case that it is impossible to understand the New Testament aright without seeing that the drama it records is that of a conflict of two kingdoms, that of God and that of the devil. The reason the Son of God appeared was to destroy the works of the devil.[1] To remove this element of conflict from the gospels would lead to a major misunderstanding of the mission of Jesus.[2]

This statement is borne out by the fact that at every level of its witness the New Testament takes the spiritual conflict seriously. The reality of spiritual powers of good are taken for granted in the gospels.[3] Against this background the reality of opposing spiritual powers is equally recognised. In the Old Testament there is considerable restraint concerning the person of Satan and he is only mentioned on three occasions.[4] The New Testament, however, presents us with a picture of a world under the domination of Satan. For instance, in the Gospel of Luke, after his baptism and anointing, Jesus is tempted by the devil (Lk 4:1–13); he very quickly encounters and delivers a demon-possessed man in the synagogue at Capernaum (Lk 4:33–37); in the midst of a healing ministry he deals frequently with the demonic (Lk 4:41); he heals a woman who has been crippled by Satan for eighteen years (Lk 13:16) and he is finally betrayed after Satan enters into Judas Iscariot (Lk 22:3). This picture of a 'powerful personal agency of evil, in whom is concentrated intense opposition to the mission of Jesus'[5] is confirmed by the Gospel of John which speaks of Satan as the 'ruler of this world' (Jn 12:31; 14:30; 16:11) who functions as the enemy of God and is a 'murderer' and 'the father of lies' (Jn 8:44). John also sees Satan as the power behind the betrayal of Jesus (13:27) and cites Jesus as saying that through his lifting up 'the prince of this world' will be driven out (12:31).

It would be possible to go on multiplying references to prove the point that in each strand of the New Testament there is a consciousness of the powers of darkness as real and malevolent entities, but it is not necessary to do so. The question is, how can we who live in a very different world from that of the New Testament, a scientific, 'enlightened' and far more sophisticated age, go on believing in the reality of such personalised powers as the devil and his demons? A number of responses are possible at this point.

1. Unconditional acceptance

It is possible to accept the picture with which the New Testament presents us quite uncritically. After all, if this is the way the New Testament teaches it then this is the way it must be whatever modern ways of thinking may make of it. This approach may have a willingness to believe the Bible and to commend it, but what it may miss is the possibility that modern understanding of the ways that individuals and societies function may in fact be able to shed light back on the teaching of the New Testament. This in turn might help us to a fuller understanding of the way the power of darkness operates. We should not underestimate the power of modern thought actually to disclose further depths in the New Testament witness and if this is the case we should be concerned to read the New Testament in the light of modern knowledge and address modern knowledge in the light of the New Testament to see what each may reveal about the other.

2. Unconditional rejection

A further response is to consign the New Testament teaching concerning the power of evil to the dustbin of history in the belief that it belongs to a world of superstition and primitive belief out of which the human race, aided by the other more positive insights of Jesus into the fatherhood of God and the brotherhood of man, is emerging. In this way of thinking the only form of darkness in the world is that which is produced by humankind's own wrong attitudes or wrong behaviour. If the New Testament symbols of the devil and the demons have any value, it is simply as an outward projection onto a cosmic screen of struggles between dark and light which are taking place within people. The real struggle is in the interior world and not in the cosmic realm which remains morally neutral. As objective entities, the devil and demons do not exist. Rather, the devil is symbolic of corporate, structural evil produced by the social structures of human society. 'Demons' are primitive ways of describing what we now know to be mental illness. Further, the old imagery of the devil is to be rejected as too simplistic, causing us to divide complicated matters into black and white.

The difficulty with maintaining this point of view is, for a Christian, twofold. Firstly, it remains a major stumbling block that Jesus himself appears to have believed in the external existence of powers of evil. It would be impossible to argue convincingly that when Jesus entered into the world of demonic conflict he was merely pretending to believe in something he knew was not real. It might be more convincing to argue that Jesus' acceptance of the devil belonged to the area of his divine accommodation to human ignorance and weakness. Becoming a man may be said to imply becoming one who shared the assumptions and beliefs of his day and of his culture. Were it not so it would have been impossible for Jesus to speak meaningfully in the context in which he lived. So, it might be argued, Jesus' apparent belief in the spiritual powers of evil is no more binding on us today than, say, the belief in a flat earth.

This line of argument is worthy of respect, if not of agreement. It attempts to take seriously what it means for Jesus to become man in space and time. Where it founders is on the centrality which the devil has in the ministry and work of Christ. On any showing it is not possible to escape the fact that Jesus believed in the reality of the devil. He was profoundly aware not just of a general belief in spirits, but of a personal conflict with such powers. The temptation narratives, which must have their origin in Jesus' own self-awareness, are testimony to this. So is his saying in Luke

10:18: 'I saw Satan fall like lightning from heaven', and his final awareness of conflict with the 'prince of this world' immediately prior to his crucifixion (Jn 12:31). It is the very centrality of this spiritual conflict to the self-awareness of Jesus which indicates that there is something here which is of the essence and far more than an incidental accommodation to human ignorance or to cultural conditions. The question must then be asked, in what sense can we speak of the Lordship of Christ, his ability to determine the shape of our existence, if we reject something which is so clearly part of his own way of believing? To do so begins to evacuate the confession of Jesus as Lord of any possible significance.

A second reason why the rejection of the New Testament witness to the powers of darkness is problematic is because to do so inevitably involves the distortion of all the other teachings which are integrally linked with it. If the enslavement of the world by the devil is the negative presupposition on which the rest of the faith is built, the presupposition cannot be altered without in the process altering that which proceeds from it. The reason the Son of God came forth was to destroy the devil's work. If we no longer believe in the devil's work we must find another reason why the Son of God came into the world. Michael Green may have a rather bald way of saying it but he hits close to the mark when he says: 'I believe the Christian doctrines of God, of man and of salvation are utterly untenable without the existence of Satan. You simply cannot write him out of the story and then imagine that the story is basically unchanged.'[6] This remark of Green's has been sharply criticised and possibly he does come near to giving the devil too honourable a place in the Christian scheme. But his basic point stands. We cannot dispose of one of the central themes in the New Testament without jeopardising the whole. It would appear that straightforward rejection of the concept of the devil does not do justice to Jesus or the New Testament, or indeed to Christian theology as a whole.

3. Sympathetic reinterpretation

Is there any mileage then in pursuing a third approach, namely the attempt to reinterpret New Testament language in a way which makes sense in the light of modern knowledge? Integral to this approach is the understanding that primitive beliefs are not necessarily wrong beliefs. It is bad practice to brand as superstition categories of thought which may appear to us to be outmoded. Rather than making the rash assumption that modern day thinking is necessarily superior to that of previous generations, we should recognise that in the process of rationalisation, industrialisation and secularisation which has so extensively shaped the modern Western world we may have lost as much as we have gained. The relentless drive to reduce everything to its basic components that we may understand and control it may in fact mean that we fail to appreciate the *wholeness* of the universe. Pursuit of reason may lead to loss of intuition, pursuit of knowledge to loss of wisdom. Modern man has much to learn from 'primitive' societies. Specifically, the language of the devil and demons may be taken as describing elements in our own human existence, the consciousness of evil, which we do not have the language to describe in any other way. Our task is to penetrate into this language, to sense what it refers to from the inside and then to find language and vocabulary which will do justice to it in our day and age.

This approach has much to commend it, not least its sympathy and humility. The question remains, however, as to whether at the end of the day it is possible to improve upon the New Testament concepts of the devil and his demons or whether any attempted reinterpretation would end up missing something of crucial importance. Perhaps there is something about evil which can only be adequately expressed in any culture and at any time by using the thought forms and the language that the New Testament gives us.

Having outlined a variety of approaches perhaps the author of this book should come clean. How am I approaching the issue? I would hope to characterise my own approach as that of 'thoughtful acceptance' of the New Testament teaching. By this I declare my conviction that we cannot rise above or beyond what we are taught by Jesus and his apostles. Rather we find that if we risk everything in the faith that what Jesus taught is true, we will not be disappointed. This is part of the scandal of Christian faith. I approach New Testament teaching therefore in the spirit of acceptance. But this acceptance is thoughtful. It proceeds on the assumption that precisely because the New Testament teaches truth, that truth will be confirmed by honest enquiry and human discovery. Modern knowledge can greatly expand our insight into what the New Testament teaches on the subject of evil by disclosing more fully how it is that the powers of darkness are at work in people and in societies. In this regard it is possible to learn from those who find the New Testament teaching difficult and search for new ways of describing evil. There is certainly a tendency for people to use 'devil' language to project their own inner struggles. All that is called devil is not therefore devil. It is possible to learn from those who would seek to reinterpret New Testament language because in so doing they may well offer clues as to how the power of darkness gains strength and exerts power in a complicated world. The New Testament needs to be read therefore in the light of such thinking, not to contradict its message but to aid understanding of its depth. In doing this the fear that the New Testament might not be able to stand up for itself belongs to the realm of unbelief and not that of faith.

To return to our original question. Should Christians believe in the devil? Anybody who has successfully followed the argument thus far might expect that we might now answer this question in the affirmative. Christians ought to believe in the devil! In fact I wish to assert the opposite. As far as Christians are concerned the devil should be the object of disbelief. Some Christians would strongly assert that a major problem of the church is that it believes insufficiently strongly in the devil. My objection is the precise opposite. We believe in the devil too much. As Christians we confess our faith in God, maker of heaven and earth, in Jesus Christ his only Son our Lord and in the Holy Spirit, the Lord and Giver of Life. We believe in God. We disbelieve in the devil.

Of course, to a certain extent I am playing with words, specifically the word 'believe'. To believe in somebody or something implies that we believe in their existence. But it also carries certain overtones of an investment of faith or trust. To believe in Jesus means more than believing in his existence. It involves personal trust and faith by virtue of which the power of Christ is magnified in the life of the believer. The access of Christ to an individual's life, his power of influence within them is in proportion to their faith. The same use of language applies in the wider world. To believe in a political leader implies more than believing in their existence; it implies faith in the system of values for which they stand.

The reply to the question, should Christians believe in the devil must therefore be a resounding No! We believe in God and on the basis of this faith we disbelieve in the devil. It is an act of disbelief which is grounded in faith. This may seem to some to be a quibble over words but it arises out of the very genuine and necessary concern that too many Christians have a big devil and a small God. The editor of the *I Believe. . .* series of books on Christian doctrine exhibited a sound instinct at this point. Having produced a series including titles such as *I Believe in Revelation*, *I Believe in the Historical Jesus* and *I Believe in the Second Coming*, he could not bring himself to call the book on the devil *I Believe in the Devil*. Instead it was called *I Believe in Satan's Downfall!* The instinct that dictated this change in the pattern was exactly right. Satan is not the object of Christian belief but of Christian disbelief. We resolutely refuse the devil place. Otto Weber has it right when he says:

> To be sure, as Christians we do not believe 'in' the devil. The devil is not mentioned in the creed. But we do believe 'against' the devil. The whole creed is simultaneously the 'renunciation' of the devil. Yet the power against which faith is faith has its own reality, just as certainly as it does not have its own validity.[7]

Weber helps us to strike a balance. We do not believe in the devil but against him and in doing so we acknowledge that the power of darkness has its own reality. It exists, but for the Christian exists as something to be rejected and denied. The importance of this consists precisely in the fact that when Christians are to be found believing 'in' the devil they succeed against their will and no doubt against their knowledge in actually increasing the devil's power.

This may be seen in several of the areas to which reference has been made in the first chapter. The great witch craze gathered momentum because people were too willing to believe in what the devil could do. In this mood they ascribed all manner of things to the devil. The power and presence of the devil thus became exaggerated because

25

people were too willing to believe. Such an attitude is not altogether lacking in the contemporary church. In giving greater focus to the reality of the power of darkness the renewal movement runs the danger of seeing the devil where he is not or of so exaggerating and heightening incidents or situations that the power of darkness is blown out of all proportion to its actual presence. When this happens it is scarcely indistinguishable from superstition. So a demon consciousness arises which bears no relation to the actual situation and which distorts and degrades the individual. This attitude can rightly be described as neurotic religion breeding a paranoid view of reality. It produces a demonised world and renders those who hold such an attitude not a little demonic themselves.

My argument is that how we think about evil is of great importance. C. S. Lewis's dictum about the two equal and opposite errors is right. We err both by disregarding the reality of evil and by taking it so seriously that we overestimate it or become overconscious of it so that it clouds our vision of God and of his world. The resolution of this problem lies not only in our refusal to be attracted by evil but also in learning to talk about it in a way which both takes it seriously and in the same breath downgrades it. The title of this book serves as a warning that even for Christians evil can present an attractive face. It fascinates us and occupies our attention. The subtitle of the book — putting the power of darkness in its place — is what we should be about. The reason this problem arises is that we are talking about a power which is inherently deceptive. According to Jesus the devil has been a liar from the beginning.[8] It is of the nature of evil to deceive and the devil has been about this task since the serpent spoke to Eve in the garden.[9] One form of deception is to persuade people to disregard his existence since this anonymity opens up many opportunities. If this strategy fails then the alternative is to exaggerate his power so that excessive fear is created which in turn allows darkness to thrive and provides a form of access for it into our lives. The Christian exists in his or her thinking within the tension of, on the one hand, not taking the devil seriously enough and thus coming into deception and, on the other hand, taking him too seriously and seeing him at work where he is not and thus falling into another form of deception. It is right models of thought that will keep our perspective clear and keep the power of darkness in its place.

Why is it that we run the risk of distortion in this area? We have already indicated that the nature of the devil is deception, falsity, untruth. When we consider the power of deception in human life we should realize what a great force this power of darkness has. Immense amounts of suffering are caused in the world because individuals have distorted images of God, of themselves and of other people leading them to treat others as enemies to be feared rather than as people to be loved. The same is true on a far grander scale of the relations between nations. If people could only see one another as they are, apart from the fears, prejudices and bigotry that are produced by the powers of deception, we would be living in quite a different world.

But other factors contribute to the distorting of our perspective on evil. There is for instance *the attraction which the power of darkness exerts*. It is a matter of indisputable fact that people are more easily attracted by evil than by the good. There is a black-hole quality that evil displays, drawing attention to itself in a way which is apparently more powerful than the good. Evil truly can display a fair face. Thus it is that it is the aberrations of human life that sell newspapers, inspire TV programmes and become the subjects of novels. Perhaps it is that evil has a certain inexplicable quality that eludes people and causes them to want to fathom the mystery. Perhaps people enjoy the vicarious thrill of reading or hearing of evil and tragedy. Whatever may be the case on the popular level, there is an attraction which evil exerts even over the minds of Christian people. The popularity of books and tapes on the demonic is not purely to be attributed to the desire for greater spiritual effectiveness. There is the unhealthy attraction of the forbidden to be reckoned with. 'Demon syndrome' is a possibility even for those who should be least attracted to the demonic and should be recognised and named as the form of spiritual pathology that it is.

Another factor which comes into play here is *the inadequacy of our human language*. Human language finds it hard to describe the nature of evil adequately. This should not surprise us as language is intended to describe the positive and wholesome realities of our human existence and not the negative and chaotic powers of evil. The result is, however, that even in our language we run the danger of being too positive about the power of darkness. Let me illustrate this by highlighting two points.

The use of *personal language* about the devil is problematic. It personalises the devil and therefore gives a dignity to him which he does not deserve. To refer to the devil as 'he' or 'him' (as we have already done frequently) confers upon the devil a form of language which strictly speaking refers to persons who are made in the image of God. It is only by analogy that it is appropriate to use the word of the devil. Its primary use is in relation to persons and it carries a sense of persons who feel, love, relate and have the dignity of personhood bestowed upon them by God. Such language is problematic in reference to the devil because it would be more accurate to think of the devil as a non-person, as subpersonal rather than personal. It would be more accurate and satisfying if we were able to refer to the devil as 'it'. This same difficulty is felt by

Andrew Walker who writes: 'For myself I would rather refer to the Devil as "it" than "him", because "him" denotes someone who is a person, or at least a being who can be said to exhibit the traits of personhood. Strictly speaking, I feel that only God is truly personal and we as human beings are only persons in so far that we can be said to bear God's image. I am not sure that we can say that about the Evil One: the Devil is all that God is not.'[10]

A further difficulty with personal language is that it denotes the kind of limitations that characterise personal individuality. We are therefore led by this language to visualize the devil as an evil individual which in turn may mean that we lose the proper sense of the pervasive nature of evil. This is not intended to suggest that the devil is omnipresent but that there is a quality about the power of darkness which is at least co-extensive with humanity. Wherever human beings are, the power of darkness lies close at hand. It may have been observed that I have exhibited thus far a marked preference for the phrase 'power of darkness' because it would seem to express more adequately both the pervasive and the non-human aspects of this reality as it is experienced by men.

Having said all of this about the problems of personal language it nevertheless appears to be impossible to speak seriously about the devil without at some point using personal language. This is partly because Jesus himself clearly used such language. Paul supplements this with the more impersonal language of the 'principalities and powers' variety suggesting the diversity of the power of darkness but like Jesus consistently refers to the devil. Because Jesus thought in terms of a conflict with an enemy which he called the devil there must have been good reason for doing so. Perhaps the reason is that if we avoid this language we miss a vital ingredient in the description of the power of darkness, namely the sense of an intelligence that is both wilful and malevolent. These points will be investigated more fully at a later point.

A further difficulty of our use of language is in the area of what is known technically as *ontology*, the study of being. To speak of the devil creates the impression that in the order of being (God–creation–angels–mankind) there is a further order of being which also has its place — the devil and his angels. The problem with this is that unwittingly a certain legitimacy is conferred upon the devil. The devil takes his place among the *dramatis personae* of the human drama and becomes a necessary, even in his own way an honoured, part of human life. The devil becomes somehow respectable and acceptable. One of the great criticisms of John Milton's epic poem *Paradise Lost* is that the devil is portrayed as a sympathetic, tragic figure in the Promethean mould. By contrast God seems distinctly boring, 'too busy being almighty to be very interesting'.[11] We need to be able to assert with Otto Weber: 'The power against which faith is faith has its own reality, *just as it certainly does not have its own validity*.' The point is that the devil has no legitimacy. He does not have a place assigned to him by God. If he exists he exists in violation of all that is right, true and legitimate. Evil cannot be assigned an acceptable place of dignity within God's universe — it has so such place, it has no right to exist. It is total and complete aberration. For this reason the devil is not something, or someone to be believed in; it is something or someone to be resolutely rejected and refused by those who believe in Christ.

Something of this attitude, one which accepts evil's existence but does not accept its validity may be discerned in the words of Jesus in Lk 10:1–20. In this chapter, Jesus sends out his disciples to be his representatives in the towns and villages and to prepare the way for his own coming. No doubt they go out in fear and in trepidation wondering what awaits them. In the event they are overjoyed at what they experience. For them the most exciting thing is that 'even the demons submit to us in your name' (v 17). Jesus quickly tells them that he has been aware of their effectiveness in this realm. 'I saw Satan fall like lightning from heaven' (v 18). He goes on to speak of the authority which he has given to them: 'I have given you authority to trample on snakes and scorpions and to overcome all the power of the enemy; nothing will harm you' (v 19). But then, significantly, he directs their attention away from the demons and back to God: 'However do not rejoice that the demons submit to you, but rejoice that your names are written in heaven' (v 20). It is almost as if Jesus is warning his disciples about the dangers of being overconcerned with or overfocused upon the demons. The source of our rejoicing is not to be the negative fact that we have power over demons but the positive fact that our names are written in heaven and we have a secure relationship and destiny in God. Not even victory over the demons is a valid source of spiritual emotion and sustenance. Encounter with the demonic either in thought or in action can quickly lead to a loss of perspective due to the mesmeric and deceptive power of darkness. The only way to maintain the perspective is to fill our horizons and hearts with the knowledge of God. Only then can we see the power of darkness for the beggarly and empty thing that it is. Christians should exercise disbelief in the devil by actively refusing to give it the credibility it keenly desires but does not deserve. The next two chapters are concerned with how we may do this more adequately.

REFERENCES

1. 1 Jn 3:8.
2. Donald Guthrie *New Testament Theology* (Leicester, 1981) p123.
3. See eg Mt 26:53; Lk 12:8; Lk 15:10.
4. Zech 3:1; Job 1–2; 1 Chron 21:1.
5. Donald Guthrie *op cit* p127.
6. Michael Green *I Believe in Satan's Downfall* (London, 1981) p20. This statement is singled out for criticism in a review of the book by Edward Ball in *Theological Renewal* **19** (1981) pp33–36.
7. Otto Weber *Foundations of Dogmatics* Vol 1 (Grand Rapids, 1981) p489.
8. Jn 8:44.
9. 1 Tim 4:1; 2 Cor 11:3.
10. Andrew Walker *Enemy Territory* (London, 1987) p10.
11. Walter Wink *op cit* p34.

—————— CHAPTER THREE ——————

Analysing Evil (I)
Its Essence

The more the devil is trivialised the easier it becomes to dismiss him. Therefore we should avoid trivialising evil. When we speak about the devil we immediately conjure up a host of images that have been passed on to us by our culture. Satan is presented as a horned satyr-like creature with a long, pointed, leering, ugly face and a three-pronged fork. Such images are drawn from pagan mythology rather than the Bible. The effect of them is to make of the devil a figure which bears no relation to life as most of us know it and who may be casually dismissed as a piece of superstitious nonsense. This represents a victory for the opposition. To be able to take evil seriously we need more sophisticated ways of understanding it.

It is significant that the Bible does not offer us crude images of the devil but rather speaks in terms of the invisible power that the devil uses. It is true to say that the devil is pictured as a serpent[1], but it is more usual for the activity of the devil to come into view. Satan is a liar and a murderer[2], a betrayer[3], a destroyer[4], an accuser and a slanderer.[5] He keeps people bound and in prison[6] and tempts to evil.[7] He is an enemy of God and of righteousness.[8] It is therefore the influence and effect of evil in the world which receive attention in the Bible rather than pictorial descriptions of the devil. This serves as a clue to how we may envisage or describe the essence of evil in the world. Properly considered, what the Bible teaches us is not a trivial, lurid piece of superstition but a sophisticated and profound description of what human beings experience in life.

This chapter seeks to penetrate more fully into the nature of evil and will do so by engaging in dialogue with three contemporary thinkers. It will be seen that none of them is regarded as giving a satisfactory analysis of the essence of evil, but each of them has something to contribute to our understanding of what evil is and how it operates. These insights will be utilised in attempting in due course to describe the essence of evil in so far as we can. In the next chapter our analysis of evil will continue with an investigation of its form.

1. Evil as Discreativity

We begin with a short examination of the American theologian Edwin P. Lewis who has taken a particular interest in the concept of the demonic.[9] Lewis began his theological pilgrimage as a liberal and moved from there to being an evangelical before taking up a Zoroastrian position. It is in Zoroastrianism with its concept of an eternal dualism, a conflict between Angra Mainyu, the principle of the lie, and Ahura Mazda, the principle of truth, that some of the background to biblical thought is to be found.[10] Lewis came to conceive of the world as being composed of three eternal existents — God (who is creative), the Adversary (who is discreative) and the Residue (which is uncreative).[11] In this way it is possible to explain the phenomena of existence. God is creatively at work in the world giving it shape and purpose. His creativity is opposed by the Adversary who continually discreates and disrupts God's creative work. The world itself is the Residue, not itself creative but being acted upon by the two opposing forces of good and evil. Mankind is therefore living in a world which is caught between these two forces and is itself free to work with the force which makes for creativity or discreativity.

There are echoes here of the concept of the Force popularised in the Star Wars trilogy. The Force is essentially one but is composed of a good side and a disruptive side. It is possible to use the Force for good or ill and mankind's choice counts in this process. Those who work with the good side of the Force can achieve a degree of spiritual enlightenment just as those who identify with the dark side can achieve a form of malevolent spirituality and power.

What can be said about Lewis (or about the Force!)? From a Christian point of view it is obvious that there is an understanding of reality here which has its own attraction. The creative–discreative–uncreative concept takes account of the actual phenomena which are at work in the world. There are forces of good and forces which oppose the good and seek to undo it wherever it is found. This is true to the sense of struggle which is characteristic of all life. If the good is to be maintained it can only be at the cost of continual output of creative energy. Where this ceases, the forces of decay and discreativity are at work. In a sense, it is easier to be discreative since nothing positive needs to be achieved — it is simply a matter of undoing what the good has done. This explains the attraction that evil has for men — it is easier to side with the forces of darkness than to expend the energy which makes for good. Sloth is of the essence of sin. This also explains how human beings can be 'good' or 'evil' and puts a value on moral decision and upon the direction of our lives.

These elements in Lewis' thought are attractive. However from the point of view of Christian theology his overall scheme must be rejected on the basis that it makes evil co-eternal with good and thereby denies the sovereignty and supremacy of the good God. If the Adversary is co-eternal with God, then God is not the God of the Christian revelation. Despite this, the concept of discreativity adds to our understanding of how evil is at work in the world seeking to discreate what God has created. The Adversary opposes the work of God and seeks to thwart it. Human beings are caught in this conflict but are able by the direction and commitment of their lives to invest in the creative or the uncreative side. These are useful concepts and expand our understanding of the nature of evil.

2. Evil and 'nothingness'

Karl Barth was the outstanding theologian of the early twentieth century and had quite definite opinions on most things. For the most part Barth's theology is a startling restatement of orthodox Christianity as understood in the Reformed tradition. In his transition from a liberal to an evangelical theology, Barth was strongly influenced by Johann Christoph Blumhardt and his son Christoph Friedrich (of whom more later). Both of these men were acquainted with the encounter with the demonic. In addition, Barth lived in Germany at the time of Hitler's rise to power and from the beginning recognised the anti-Christian nature of National Socialism, unlike the majority of his fellow Christians. He was inclined to take seriously the power of evil in a way which many other theologians did not and in doing so developed a quite distinct concept of evil as 'nothingness' (*Das Nichtige*).

The concept of nothingness needs to be understood within the context of Barth's theology as a whole. It is characteristic that he attempts to escape from static categories of thought and to conceive of God and his work in dynamic terms. The concept of nothingness is Barth's attempt to conceive of a power in opposition to God that has a negatively dynamic character. He freely admits that the term is one that he has fashioned himself and is therefore to be taken with a grain of salt. It does however express briefly, tersely and strongly insights which are truly biblical.[13] It is not his intention to suggest that evil does not exist but that it exists in negativity, without any right to exist, without any value or positive strength. Its nature is perversion.[14] The fact of nothingness (that is to say of evil) is revealed through Christ in the sense that the hostility of nothingness to God is revealed in its hostility to Christ. At the same time nothingess is under God's control and Christ's incarnation is God's answer to it.[15] Nothingness takes form as real death, real devil, real hell and the real sin of man.[16]

> In Him, ie, in contradistinction to Him, nothingness is exposed in its entirety as the adversary which can destroy both body and soul in hell, as the evil one which is also the destructive factor of evil and death that stands in sinister conflict against the creature and its creator, not merely as an idea which man may conceive and to which he can give allegiance but as the power which invades and subjugates and carries him away captive, so that he is wholly and utterly lost in the face of it.[17]

Barth insists that our knowledge of this evil reality is not a matter of speculation but a clear deduction from the self-disclosure of God in Jesus Christ.

> It is not a speculation but a description which even the veriest child can understand simply to say of evil in the

first instance that it is what God does not will. But to say this is also to say that it is something which He never did nor could will, nor ever will nor can. It is thus that evil is characterised, judged and condemned in the self-disclosure of the living person of Jesus Christ. As opposition to God, it is that which is simply opposed to His will, and from eternity, in time and to all eternity negated, rejected, condemned and excluded by his will.[18]

The term 'nothingness' can be seen therefore to have value in that it attempts to describe the essence of evil. Evil is that about which nothing positive can be said or thought. It exists in negation and is itself wholly negative. This must pose the question, how then can such a power exist in a world that God has made? Where is its origin? At this point we begin to push beyond the limits of the human capacity to understand. The traditional doctrine has been that evil has its origin in the free will of men and of angels. It is the freedom of angels and men to go astray that is the point at which evil originates in a good universe. However Barth resists such an idea. The concept of a pre-mundane angelic fall is rejected scathingly as 'one of the bad dreams of the older dogmatics'.[19] He rejects the idea because, in his book, angels do not and cannot fall. The devil was never an angel but a liar and a murderer from the beginning.[20] Verses in the Bible which seem to point in the direction of an angelic fall are too uncertain and obscure to build upon.[21] Nothingness is an alien factor which can be attributed neither to the positive will and work of God nor to the activity of the creature.[22] Yet neither can it exist independently of the will of God since this would be to deny his Lordship.[23]

We are confronted here with a genuine difficulty in understanding. Nothingness is real. It is not nothing and yet it has nothing in common with God or his creatures.

It must therefore exist in a third way peculiar to itself. In this sense only, nothingness 'is'.[24] At this point Barth is keen to stress the invalid nature of evil. It has no right to exist as if it were a creature of God or on the same terms. Its existence is not a planned and willed existence as is that of mankind. We are faced here with something that is real but has no right to be.

Barth further rejects the idea of an angelic fall because he resents the equation of angels and demons. He sees the association of the two in much theology as 'primitive and fatal'.[25] He takes great delight in the subject of angels and deals with them in a novel and creative way with the intention of restoring to them 'permanent residence visas' in Christian theology.[26] The best way to describe his under-standing of angels is to see them as beings which are summoned into existence wherever God is at work among men. They are witnesses of God who precede, accompany, surround and follow the coming kingdom of God.[27] Angels 'slip between our fingers' because they are free from any personal desire for power or lordship. They belong fully to God and in no sense to themselves.[28] Because of this and unlike human beings angels cannot deviate. Therefore they cannot become fallen creatures.

In this context Barth turns his attention to the demons, the opponents of the ambassadors of God. He finds this subject distasteful and therefore is only willing to cast 'a momentary glance' at the demons. Because demons thrive on attention and to contemplate them too intensely raises the danger that we too may become a little demonic, a quick, sharp glance is all that is necessary and legitimate.[29] The demons exist in a 'dreadful fifth or sixth dimension of existence' and are constantly active 'like the tentacles of an octopus'.[30] They exist as an army never in repose and always on the march invading and attacking with falsehood as their manner of being.[31]

According to Barth then, we cannot look for the origin of evil in a supposed fall of angels. Where then is such an origin to be found? Here Barth is at his most novel. Nothingness, he argues, has its origin in the 'No' of God which is implied by his original, creative 'Yes'. In other words, in saying 'Yes' to the creation and calling it into being, God uttered an implied 'No', a rejection of that which is evil, and this 'No', being also a powerful word of God, has created the realm of nothingness. Nothingness is that which God rejects, opposes, negates and dismisses in the act of creation.[32]

> Nothingness is that which God does not will. It lives only by the fact that it is that which God does not will. But it does live by this fact. For not only what God wills, but what He does not will, is potent and must have a real correspondence. What really corresponds to that which God does not will is nothingness.[33]

Exegetically, Barth roots his case in the chaos of Genesis 1:2. When it affirms 'the earth was formless and empty, darkness was over the surface of the deep', this is the chaos of nothingness which God despised in his creative work, the lower sphere that God passed by without a halt. It is the sphere of chaos which behind God's back has assumed the self-contradictory character of reality.[34]

What are we to make of these remarkable mental gymnastics? In support of Barth we must recognise his originality in formulating a new theory of the origin of evil. He is seeking to understand how evil can exist in a way which is contrary to the will of God but nevertheless is in the sphere of the will of God. In doing so he maintains fully the objective reality of evil, of the devil and of demons, although he rejects the concept of a fall of angels as giving too much dignity to the devil.

But perhaps Barth's greatest strength is the evident contempt for evil and the demonic which he demonstrates. The word 'nothingness' is novel, but it expresses the nature of evil as a negative force and the fact that it exists improperly in a way which is not planned or purposed by God. It is abhorred and abhorrent. The crucial conclusion drawn from this is that evil exists parasitically. It draws its energy from that which exists authentically by the will of God by sucking out the life of that which God has created. It draws its existence from the living creation on which it trades. The significance of this understanding of evil will be investigated in other contexts. It should be noted here that this concept of evil as parasite is deeply rooted in Christian thought. Augustine saw evil as *privatio boni*, an absence of goodness rather than a creature in its own right. This conforms to the concept of discreativity which we have already noted. Evil cannot create; it can only feed on or destroy that which is created. Here again is a reason why Christians should practise disbelieving in the devil. When demons or the devil get undue attention from Christians they welcome it. It is a way in which they themselves are boosted. It is a form of energy which they absorb into themselves and which enables them to go on feeding off the human energy from which they exist. Barth's concept of nothingness has therefore much to commend it in describing the essence of evil.

We cannot, however, follow Barth in his attempt to explain how evil has come to be. He must be criticised on the one hand for his use of Scripture. His use of the chaos in Genesis 1:2 as proof of his theory can only be described as a classic exegesis whereby he discovers his own theory of evil in the biblical account of creation.[35] Barth is presenting rich ideas but they have nothing to do with the text. Genesis 1:1–2 is a bald statement to the effect that God made the world out of nothing, not an attempt to explain the origin of evil.[36] Equally, Barth dismisses in a cavalier fashion the texts that appear to indicate an angelic fall. The result of this is that his concept of the origin of nothingness has more the character of a speculation than an exposition of biblical truth.[37]

Barth's concept must also be criticised for its theological inadequacy. If God himself gives rise to nothingness by virtue of the No! implied by his creative Yes!, we must ask the question, was it God's will that his No! should have this effect, or was God powerless to prevent it happening? In either case we are left with a problem. Either God wills evil and gives rise to it (in which case his goodness is compromised) or he does not will it yet is powerless to prevent it happening (in which case his sovereignty is compromised). To argue as Barth does that it is precisely God's non-willing that gives rise to nothingness must be described as a 'curiously far-fetched and concocted notion'.[38] Furthermore, Barth runs the danger of having explained too much. If evil is to be seen as something absurd and inexplicable then there is a sense in which it must defy explanation. Barth's concept renders sin and evil not so much absurd as inevitable.

We are compelled to conclude that Barth's concept does not stand up to scrutiny. At the same time he has given the analysis of evil some unusually valuable attention and the concept of nothingness is well suited to a description of the essence of evil. The realism and yet contempt with which he casts his short, sharp glance at the demonic kingdom should be taken as a model for those who reflect on this subject. In the next chapter an alternative understanding of the origin of evil will be attempted which is more in accord with the traditional position. But as with the concept of discreativity, Barth's concept of nothingness will be pressed into service in the attempt to state a more adequate analysis of the nature of evil.

3. Evil and 'interiority'

A wide-ranging and highly perceptive study of this whole area is currently being attempted by American theologian Walter Wink.[39] This work deserves a great deal of attention because of the insights that it offers into the nature of evil. Wink takes the biblical witness concerning the devil, demons, and principalities and powers with the utmost seriousness and finds the language of spiritual power pervading the New Testament.

> On every page of the New Testament one finds the terminology of power: those incumbents, offices, structures, roles, institutions, ideologies, rituals, agents and spiritual influences by which power is established and exercised.[40]

To do justice to this dimension of human experience, we need to have an appropriate terminology. In the Bible this is found by the use of such terms as the devil, demons etc. Therefore far from being primitive such language is actually highly sophisticated in describing life as it is. When confronted with certain experiences we find it difficult to avoid such words as 'satanic' or 'demonic' in order to describe them adequately. These concepts cannot be reduced to merely psychological or sociological entities, since to do this is to miss completely the spiritual dimension to reality.[41] Yet the mythological language of the Bible needs to be reinterpreted. As far as Wink is concerned the 'Powers' do not have a separate spiritual existence from the earthly reality through which they become manifest. The spiritual powers are to be understood as the 'innermost essence' of earthly realities. To illustrate:

[A] 'mob spirit' does not hover in the sky waiting to leap

43

down on an unruly crowd at a football match. It is
the actual spirit constellated when the crowd reaches a
certain critical flashpoint of excitement and frustration.
It comes into existence in that moment, causes people
to act in ways of which they would not have dreamed
themselves capable, and then ceases to exist at the
moment the crowd disperses.[42]

This concept of the innermost essence Wink proposes to
call 'interiority' and he sees it as being necessary to explain
the realities of human existence. His thesis is that 'the
New Testament's "principalities and powers" is a generic
category referring to the determining forces of physical,
psychic and social existence. These powers usually consist
of an outer manifestation and an inner spirituality or
interiority.'[43]

In developing his thinking, Wink then goes on to apply
his concept of 'interiority' to the specific features of the
New Testament witness. Satan, for instance, 'did not begin
life as an idea, but in experience'.[44] The context for Satan
is that of an actual encounter with something or someone
that leads to the positing of his existence. What is this
encounter?

Wink points here to an ambiguity in the Bible's witness.
In the Old Testament Satan especially is described as a
servant of God and has the role of an agent provocateur
or of a public prosecutor. He functions as an adversary, as
'that actual inner or collective voice of condemnation that
any sensitive person hears tirelessly repeating accusations
of guilt or inferiority'.[45] In sections of the New Testament
Satan is portrayed as 'God's holy sifter' and sometimes as
God's 'enforcer', called in to work us over when more
gentle methods will not succeed.

When God cannot reach us through our conscious

commitment, sometimes there is no other way to get our attention than to use the momentum of our consciousness to slam us up against the wall. Heavenly jujitsu, practised by God's 'enforcer', this meat-fisted, soul-sifting Satan — servant of the living God![47]

In all of these roles Satan is actually useful and, according to Wink, is not evil personified but rather the one who offers us choices and thereby tests us and helps us to develop in conscious obedience to God by refusing the possibilities to which he points. Wink's view of Satan is that 'the conscious devil is useful; the unconscious devil is perilous'[48] meaning by this that if we are aware what is happening then we are consciously able to refuse the temptation. If we are not aware we are in trouble. Because of the usefulness of the devil in this regard he argues that Satan has been persistently maligned. The devil is not all bad. It needs to be noted that although he uses the language of 'Satan' and 'the devil', Wink has actually demythologised the biblical concepts and reinterpreted them in terms of interiority while attempting to remain true to the sense of encounter with evil. In other words, the devil as an independent entity does not exist but has been absorbed into the interiority of human experiences.

How then does Satan, the servant of God, become the Evil One, the Enemy of God, the Father of Lies, the Black One, the Archfiend of Christian theology? Wink points to the fact that agents provocateurs have a tendency to overstep their mandate and that Satan appears to have 'evolved from a trustworthy intelligence-gatherer into a virtually autonomous and invisible suzerain within a world ruled by God'.[49] He opens up for us here the intriguing possibility that Satan may originally have been created by God to exercise his 'sifting' role within creation but has gone too far in the exercise of his provocative role. The 'fall of Satan' could therefore be regarded as an attempt to push the boat out too far. Wink however cannot mean this literally because Satan has no independent existence. Satan's fall, for him, did not take place in time or in the universe in any external sense but in the human psyche.[50] By man's rejection of God, Satan has become 'the symbolic repository of the entire complex of evil existing in the present order'.[51] Because Wink defines the powers as interiority he must seek for a shift towards evil in this realm not in some theological fall of angels but in the interior life of humanity, that is in human sin. Satan is the expression of the corporate interiority of such a fallen race.

> Satan is the real interiority of a society that idolatrously pursues its own enhancement as the highest good. Satan is the spirituality of an epoch, the peculiar constellation of alienation, greed, inhumanity, oppression and entropy that characterises a specific period of history as a consequence of human decisions to tolerate and even further such a state of affairs.[52]

There is no doubt that for those who wish to investigate this realm in the future, Wink's books will be essential reading. As with the other thinkers who have been reviewed in this chapter there will be a point at which disagreement becomes necessary but there is much to learn from Wink's approach. Several areas in particular are worth further comment.

(i) All the time he is seeking to work out his understanding in the light of the Bible's teaching and in particular in speaking of Satan he seeks to do justice to the role Satan appears to play as a servant of God, particularly in the Old Testament. There is a marked tendency in the Old Testament to ascribe evil directly to God.[53] The New

Testament is far more 'dualist' in the sense of recognising the activity of an evil power in the world which although not inspired by God is nevertheless under God's control. Wink's account of Satan as an agent provocateur who oversteps the mark is thus an intriguing insight. As we will see, however, it is not the only way of interpreting the data.

(ii) Wink offers a highly sophisticated analysis of evil which is credible both in terms of human experience and of the New Testament's concern with the power that opposes God. In particular his analysis illuminates the way in which evil is actually operative. He therefore moves away from an overpersonalised portrayal of evil whereby evil spirits 'hover in the air' without reference to the actual structures within which human beings fulfil their existence. Instead he posits a situation whereby evil manifests itself in the realities of human life and society. More than this, he indicates how it may be that evil actually draws its negative strength and energy by preying upon the energy of sin which is to be found in humankind and human society. This should be regarded as a highly significant insight. The devil is only as strong as human beings allow him to be. In referring to James 4:7, 'Submit yourselves therefore to God. Resist the devil and he will flee from you', he makes the point that far from being omnipotent, the devil knows his place and can be resisted.[54] Putting it baldly, the power of darkness grows in strength and energy as human beings invest their lives, their time and their attention in it. Thus, as the human race expands in size and involvement in personal and corporate sin, so the power of darkness grows. Conversely, when the opposite is the case and humans shun sin so the power of darkness is weakened because its only power is the power of deception and its ability to draw its own energy from disordered, disorientated and degraded humanity. The power of darkness cannot therefore be overcome by purely 'spiritual' means. Binding the devil, rebuking the devil, engaging in spiritual warfare will not avail if the supply lines of sin which enable the power of darkness to replenish itself parasitically from the human race are not also dealt with.

Unlike Wink, we do not consider that the devil can be denied some form of independent existence. But we do follow his train of thought in saying that the vitality of the devil is parasitic and his strength substantially drawn from humanity. It depends upon the credibility and attention that is given to him as well as on the ignorance that enables him to do his work. The power that the devil has in himself is far far less than we might imagine and far more dependent on that which mankind gives him. Essentially its power is that of deception which enables it to win men and women over to its side. The effect of this must inevitably be that in the fight with evil in which we are engaged we must pay more attention to depriving Satan of sustenance by working for the personal and social salvation of humanity. Correspondingly we need to expose and confound the lies with which the darkness enthralls and captivates humans.

(iii) We must further disagree with Wink in the overpositive picture he paints of Satan. Wink is falling victim to the fair face of evil. Satan is in his view valuable as a servant of God and is worthy of respect in that role. The problem with this approach is that Satan begins to be assimilated to God himself. Wink quotes with approval the following story of a dialogue between Sidney Harris and his daughter.

My little nine-year-old girl said to me, 'Daddy, there's something peculiar about the whole story of God and the devil and hell. It just doesn't hold together'. 'Oh', I said, 'and why doesn't it hold together?' 'Well' she continued, 'God is supposed to love good people and the devil is supposed to favour bad people. Right? The good people go to God, but the bad people go to hell, where the devil punishes them forever. Isn't that the story?' When I agreed that it was, she continued, 'It doesn't make sense. In that case the devil couldn't be the enemy of God. I mean, if the devil really was on the side of the bad people, he wouldn't punish them in hell, would he? He'd treat them nicely and be kind to them for coming over to his side. He'd give them candy and presents and not burn them up'. 'You've got a point', I said. 'So how do you work it out?' She thought for a moment and then she asserted, 'It seems to me that if the whole story is true, then the devil is secretly on the side of God, and is just pretending to be wicked. He works for God as a kind of secret agent, testing people to find out who's good or bad, but not really fighting against God'. 'That's remarkable', I exclaimed. 'Do you think there's any proof?' 'Well', she concluded, 'here's another thing. If God is really all-powerful, no devil would have a chance against him. So, if a devil really exists, it must be because he's secretly in cahoots with God!'[55]

These words of wisdom from a nine-year-old child confirm Wink in his opinion! The problem is that according to this train of thought evil ceases to be evil and begins to become partly good. With this we are in danger of losing a sense of abhorrence at evil by treating it as part of God's plan. In a later chapter this issue will be investigated further but for the moment it is sufficient to indicate that there is another way of dealing with the biblical evidence of Satan as both servant and enemy of God. Instead of asserting with Wink that he is a servant who has the potential to become an enemy because of the decisions of humanity, it is possible to assert that he is an enemy who, against his will, finds himself doing the work of a servant. It is not therefore that Satan has a legitimate place and role in human experience, but rather that the illegitimate and invalid activity of Satan is even so taken up by God and through God's creative sovereignty alone, made to serve the purposes of God. Satan is not and never will be a friend of humanity, but there is a God who is able to make the activity of Satan serve an ultimately good, though distant, purpose.

Although we have found important points of disagreement with each of the thinkers with whom we have been in dialogue, we have also found that each of them offers important insights which contribute towards a more perceptive understanding of the nature of evil. Many standard ideas that Christians have of the power of darkness serve only to trivialise it and thus to make it easy to reject. We need therefore to construct an understanding of evil which is so authentic in what it describes that it must be taken seriously. The concept of a discreative adversary helps towards this. The concept of nothingness futher helps to comprehend the negative manner of existence and activity of this discreative power. The concept of interiority helps us to see how this power is at work, not 'up in the air' in the sense of being separate from the matrix of life, but in the earthly realities with which we are familiar and where the battle rages and to which there is a spiritual, invisible dimension. It is in this way that evil gathers its energy and strength. It is with the reality of evil in this sphere that we are called to wrestle. We do not wrestle against flesh and blood but it is over flesh and blood that the invisible battle is fought and it is flesh and blood that makes itself available to the invisible powers that afflict their existence. Having attempted to express something of the essence and nature of evil we will now attempt to analyse its form. In the course of this we hope to utilise some of the insights gained up to this point.

REFERENCES

1. Gen 3:1; Rev 20:2.
2. Jn 8:44; Acts 5:3.
3. Lk 22:3.
4. 1 Pet 5:8.
5. Rev 12:10.
6. Lk 13:16.
7. 1 Cor 7:5.
8. Mt 13:39; Acts 13:10.
9. Lewis' position is summarized in Vernon R. Mallow *The Demonic: A Selected Theological Study* (New York, 1983).
10. *Evangelical Dictionary of Theology* (Basingstoke, 1985) p736.
11. Mallow *op cit* p219.
12. Barth's discussion of this theme can be found in *Church Dogmatics* (Edinburgh, 1956–75) Vol III/3 pp289–368, 519–531. A useful summary may be found in John Hick *Evil and the God of Love* (London, 1966) pp132–204.
13. *Church Dogmatics* (CD) IV/3/1 p178.
14. ibid.
15. CD III/3 p302.
16. ibid.
17. CD III/3 p312.
18. CD IV/3/1 p177.
19. CD III/3 p531.
20. ibid.
21. ibid p530 with reference to Is 14:12; Gen 6:1–14; Jude 6; 2 Pet 2:4.
22. CD III/3 p292.
23. ibid.
24. ibid p349.
25. ibid p519.
26. ibid p416.
27. ibid p457.
28. ibid p450.
29. ibid p579.
30. ibid pp527–528.
31. ibid p525.
32. ibid pp351–352.
33. ibid.

34. CD III/1 p108.
35. John Hick *op cit* p140 note 2.
36. Gerhard von Rad *Genesis* (London, 1961) p51.
37. See on this G. C. Berkouwer *The Triumph of Grace in the Theology of Karl Barth* (London, 1956) p378.
38. Helmut Thielicke *Theological Ethics* Vol I (Grand Rapids, 1979) p114.
39. See his trilogy on The Powers *Naming the Powers* (Philadelphia, 1984); *Unmasking the Powers* (Philadelphia, 1986); *Engaging the Powers* (forthcoming).
40. Wink *Naming the Powers* p99.
41. ibid p103.
42. ibid p105.
43. Wink *Unmasking the Powers* p4.
44. ibid p10.
45. ibid p12. See 2 Sam 24:1; 1 Chr 21:1; Zech 3:1–5.
46. ibid.
47. ibid p15 with reference to Lk 22:31–34; 1 Chr 5:1–5.
48. ibid p19.
49. ibid p23. See Mt 13:19; Jn 12:31; Eph 2:2; 2 Cor 6:15; Mt 10:25; 2 Cor 4:4; 1 Cor 10:10.
50. ibid p24.
51. ibid.
52. ibid p25.
53. See Ex 4:24–26; 1 Sam 16:14–16.
54. Wink *Unmasking the Powers* p21.
55. ibid p22.

───────── CHAPTER FOUR ─────────

Analysing Evil (II)
Its Form

In attempting to analyse the essence of evil in the previous chapter we found help from various thinkers of the present and the recent past. At the same time we found it necessary to disagree with some of their perspectives feeling that they were either clearly unbiblical or inadequately biblical. In this chapter the task which awaits us is that of offering an alternative perspective on evil. We will approach this by giving attention to the form of evil as this is spoken of in the Bible. It will be evident in the course of doing so that some of the insights gained in the previous chapter will be useful in this. The approach here will be to set out ten steps each of which will enable us to penetrate more fully into an analysis of the form of evil.

1. Step one

Evil is known in its most obvious and concrete form in the sinful behaviour of human beings. The Christian analysis of mankind is that we are fallen and that there is an immense gulf between what we ought to be and what we are. The narrative of the Fall in Genesis 3 is an attempt to describe the truth not only about the first man and woman, but about mankind generally and each person in particular. Adam did what all of us do. We rebel against God and fail to rise in obedient response to his love and grace. No attempt to describe the origin of sin is valid if it seeks to lessen the guilt of mankind. Yet it is clear that humans are both the perpetrators of sin and its victims. They are sinners and are sinned against. As perpetrators of sin we are objects of the divine wrath. As its victims we are the objects of the divine compassion. By itself mankind is neither clever enough nor sufficiently demonic to be the originator of evil. We are tempted by a power that is beyond us and which pre-exists us. This is indicated in Genesis 3 by the presence in the garden of the snake which poses the possibility of rejecting God's command. The snake could of course function here as a symbol of the lower nature to which mankind gives way. But the New Testament interprets it in terms of an external tempting power which it calls in Revelation 20:2: 'that ancient serpent, who is the devil, or Satan'. In understanding the form of evil we need therefore to see that it takes form in the sin of man but is not exhausted by it. We are directed beyond man towards a suprahuman power. Emil Brunner puts it likes this:

> What is evident is this: that in this classic description of the Fall, there is already a force of temptation outside man which suggests evil to man. This means that man did not himself invent evil. Man is too small, too weak, too closely connected with his senses to be the inventor of evil.[1]

This leads us to the second step in the analysis.

2. Step two

Mankind is assailed by powers greater than itself and is their victim. These greater powers are described in the Bible in a variety of ways. For instance, the apostle Paul speaks of sin as if it were a superhuman influence[2], refers to the seductive power of the law in a similar way[3] and speaks of the cosmic realm of 'principalities and powers'[4] with which mankind is in conflict. The nature of the 'powers' which are outside mankind and greater than it, is much debated in recent theology. No doubt the reason for this is that they provide modern thinkers with the opportunity to find in Scripture an area which has distinct contemporary relevance, namely the influence of socio- logical and cultural structures upon the individual. The suggestion has been put forward that whereas the demons of the gospels are the supposed causes of afflictions now treated by physicians and psychiatrists, the principalities and powers correspond to the concerns of politicians and sociologists, namely the corporate structures of human society.[5] The debate concerning the powers embraces a spectrum of opinion which is inclined at one end to identify them as angelic powers and human social structures but nothing sinister[6], and at the other end to see them as distinct supernatural agencies of a personal and sinister kind.[7] Those who stand in the middle find an absence of distinction between the two; that is to say, the references in the New Testament to powers, thrones, authorities, elemental spirits and the like are deemed to be thoroughly ambiguous, encompassing both human structures and a transcendent dimension involving spiritual powers of good and evil kinds.[8]

The subject of the powers will be discussed more thoroughly in a later chapter. Our concern at this point is simply to demonstrate the reality of suprapersonal forces to which mankind is vulnerable and which include the religious, intellectual, moral and political forces under whose influence humanity exists. Hendrik Berkhof asserts that in addition to the interpersonal, human dimensions of sin:

> We must distinguish a suprapersonal aspect which is based not so much on the mentality of persons as on the driving force inherent both in the institutions of our established society and in the anonymous powers of current modes of behaviour, taboos, traditions or the dictates of fashion. Of course both aspects hang together. First personal sin broadens itself assuming an interpersonal shape and then, continuing, it concentrates or institutionalises itself in suprapersonal magnitudes. It is the experience of those who manage to wrest themselves free from being blinded by interpersonal forces to take up the challenge of love, that individual good will seems to accomplish little or nothing against all those forces which inexorably dictate to individuals a certain pattern of conduct — the business, the interest of the party, the needs of society, custom, fashion, public opinion, the ideology (Western or Eastern) etc. One who tries to do something against it is usually thrown aside or gets crushed under the wheels. Very few possess the strength and the courage to take this risk.[9]

So we proceed to the third step.

3. Step three

The reality of the powers, the invisible dimensions of reality which influence human beings and are greater than them, enhances our understanding of human society and of how evil may be operative within it in a suprapersonal way.

But further clarification is necessary as to how it is that powers which are created by God and are part of his good creation[10] can become distorted and evil. In this step of the argument we need to make reference to the 'demonic'. It is widely recognised by Christian theologians that there is an irrational, surd-like power at work in human society which threatens and distorts existence, an alien power of deceit 'out of which have poured into human existence incredible forces of disintegration and destruction'.[11] These forces create 'a sense of helplessness in the face of some movements or situations for which no-one seems directly responsible and which no-one seems able to control'.[12] The element of the demonic has therefore re-emerged as a valid concept in much modern theology. In a work first published in 1963, Paul Tillich writes:

> The symbol of the demonic does not need justification as it did thirty years ago, when it was reintroduced into theological language. It has become a much-used and much-abused term to designate antidivine forces in individual and social life.[13]

It must also be said that different theologians mean different things by the term. But its use is a recognition of the fact, which accords with the Bible, that evil is not adequately described unless we make reference to an irrational and malevolent force at work in the world which actively causes things to go wrong.

4. Step four

To make sense of the demonic however requires us to take a further step. It is congenial to the modern mind to speak of the demonic in impersonal terms since it enables us to recognise the existence of irrational evil while avoiding the problematic and pictorial language associated with the idea of 'the devil'. Yet at the core of the Christian revelation, as we have already had cause to note, in the ministry of Jesus and at the cross the superhuman power of darkness which enslaves humanity and which is the very presupposition of the cross is represented as 'the devil' or 'Satan'.[14] The theological difficulty we encounter here and to which we have already referred, is that of speaking about the power of darkness in personal and individual terms. We need to recognise the limits of our language at this point. We are speaking symbolically, partially and not definitively.[15] On the other hand the concept of the devil has a metaphorical and direct force in expressing the relentless power of evil, the overpowering threat to mankind. To substitute any other concept somehow fails to capture the nature of the threat. Further, the devil concept captures the personal or quasi-personal nature of sin as pride and rebellion and maintains the spiritual nature of this adversary. This serves to capture the biblical insight that the highest reaches of sin are not to do with the body so much as with the spirit. The thoroughly evil nature of the devil consists in the fact that here we have spontaneous, self-generating sin expressed in pure defiance and pure arrogance.[16]

There is no sense in which the devil is a victim of an evil power which is greater than himself. He is the originator of evil and only a power which is spiritual and in some sense personal can be this point of origin. We cannot get rid of the devil from Christian understanding without radically shifting the biblical analysis. The fact that it is impossible to do justice to the reality of this power without recourse to personal language is itself an indication that only in this way can it be properly understood. Even Barth who chose to speak of evil as nothingness in order to avoid giving the impression that it had a positive form of being, found it difficult to avoid personal language.[17] When we fail to do this, reluctant though we should be to dignify the devil with personal language, we run the risk of making the power of evil so abstract that our talk loses its compelling force and clarity.

5. Step five

If then there is such a power as the devil, the question must now be asked, what is its origin? A word of caution is necessary at this point. The Bible does not give a clear answer to this question. We should therefore assume that there will be an element of uncertainty in our answer. We will see under step seven why this uncertainty exists. In attempting to explain the origin of evil there are five possible answers which we need to consider.

(a) The first is that of **metaphysical dualism.** This is the belief that the conflict between God and Satan is an eternal one. The devil exists as God's 'opposite number', with God having slightly the upper hand. The battle wages now one way, now another. This is the view expressed, as we have seen, by Edwin P. Lewis, although Lewis held open the possibility of an ultimate victory of God over the Adversary. His namesake, C. S. Lewis, was of the opinion that 'next to Christianity Dualism is the manliest and most sensible creed on the market'.[18] He said this because at least dualism recognises the element of conflict between good and evil. But it has a catch in it. Basically, this concept is one which belongs firmly outside the Christian faith. From a Christian point of view it is to be rejected as a denial of the supremacy of God. It is true to say that the New Testament contains a form of dualism, a conflict between good and evil. But it is a temporary one and not eternal. To make the devil into God's opposite number is to give him a status he does not have. This point of view runs the danger of 'domesticating' evil by making it part of the eternal order. It therefore loses the sense of the horror and unacceptability of evil.

(b) A second point of view is known as **monism.** This view goes to the opposite extreme to that of dualism by perceiving everything that happens, including evil, as being directly attributable to the will of God. If evil therefore exists, it is because God has directly willed it. There is no such thing as the permissive will of God which allows things to be which he does not strictly will. Instead, everything that is exists because God directly wills that it should be so. There is one cause for everything, namely, the will of God.

It is difficult to see how this point of view can avoid making God directly the author and originator of evil, in which case we are left with immense problems concerning the goodness of God. The monist position has been typical of High Calvinism with its strict theocentrism which refuses to give room to any lesser cause than God in the affairs of the universe. This position has been able to appeal for support to some biblical texts[19] and to some statements in the works of John Calvin, for instance:

> For the first man fell because the Lord had judged it to be expedient; why he so judged is hidden from us. . . Accordingly, man falls according as God's providence ordains, but he falls by his own fault.[20]

To take the monist position would appear to make a nonsense of God's hostility to evil and to turn the idea of grace into a farce.

(c) A third option, then, would be simply **to deny that it is possible to explain the origin of sin** on the basis that

Scripture does not speak to this particular issue or if it does, does so only in peripheral texts which are not easy to interpret. Emil Brunner, for instance, is strong in his acceptance of the reality of the devil because at the centre of the biblical revelation, especially in the life and cross of Jesus this is to be easily perceived. But he argues that in the Bible the power of darkness is simply there, and we do well not to speculate on its origin, since this is left opaque. The existence of the devil is accepted but left undefined and unaccounted for.[21] From this point of view agnosticism is better than speculation.

(d) A fourth option is to suggest, with Barth, that **evil has to do with the very structure of created reality.** Evil is there in the act of creation as the reverse side of this positive creative activity. Therefore the world in which we live is a good world as such but it is threatened by nothingness which exists as a negative power. We have already discussed the problems which are involved in this point of view and lead to its rejection.[22]

(e) Having investigated the former options we are left with the possibility of locating evil not in the structure of created reality but in the misuse of a creaturely freedom. This is in fact the traditional understanding of the church which has argued for the freedom of man and has associated evil with man's ability to contradict the will of God and go his own way. But under step two we have already indicated that the origin of evil is not in man who is insufficiently clever to give rise to it. We need therefore to seek the origin of evil in a transcendent sphere by positing a focus of misusable freedom in that dimension. Sin and evil originate in an aberration within the sphere of created reality. Man is not the originator of evil but rather has become implicated in an existing rebellion of a spiritual, suprahuman power which is responsible for purely spontaneous, self-generated sin.

6. Step six

It is clear that with this suggestion we are approaching the doctrine traditionally known as the fall of angels, the idea of a pre-mundane, angelic catastrophe. This is a concept which Barth has decisively excluded, despite the fact that he occasionally uses language reminiscent of it.[23] Barth rejected the idea that an angel could fall because he denied freedom to them. Their existence was identical with their obedience. They lacked autonomy and therefore the possibility of rebellion. Brunner likewise finds fault with the doctrine, seeing no direct scriptural basis for it. The idea of a fall of angels exists for him only on the fringe of the biblical testimony, is a relic of Persian religion and does not belong to the centre of Christian faith. Moreover it has proven to be a happy hunting ground for the imaginations of the fanatical.[24]

Before pronouncing in favour of the idea of an angelic fall, the force of these criticisms needs to be felt. In so far as the Bible speaks of an angelic fall it is certainly only obliquely and on the margins of scripture. All the texts concerned are problematic. The Old Testament passages to which appeal is sometimes made, Ezekiel 28:1–17 and Isaiah 14:12–21, can only be cited in an indirect sense since their direct reference is to identifiable human persons.[25] It is more likely that what these verses contain are heightened descriptions of historical persons than attempts to describe the origin of Satan.[26] At best, it takes a major leap of biblical interpretation to refer them to a transcendental personage.

The New Testament texts, Jude 6 and 2 Peter 2:4, are more substantial, but even so are both elusive in character.

Jude 6 speaks of 'angels who did not keep their positions of authority but abandoned their own home'. 2 Peter 2:4 refers to the fact that: 'God did not spare angels when they sinned but sent them to hell.' If we accept Jude 6 as teaching concerning an angelic fall are we also bound to accept the account in verse 9 about Michael disputing with the devil about the body of Moses, or verse 14 about Enoch's prophecies? Neither of these latter incidents are found in the Old Testament but belong to Jewish extra-biblical literature. It is possible therefore that Jude is simply using known Jewish traditions to illustrate his point rather than laying down authoritative teaching. 2 Peter 2:4 must also be seen as problematic. The 'angels that sinned' appears to be a reference to the heavenly beings in Genesis 6:1–14 who lusted after earthly women. The fate of these angels became a subject of speculation in Jewish thought.[27] If this is so, then these angels appear to have fallen after the creation of mankind and not before it. Even so, it may be that these are references to known tradition meant simply to illustrate the writer's theme of the danger of disobedience rather than intended to disclose information concerning a fall of angels.

The aim of these remarks is not to disqualify these verses from yielding up teaching concerning the origin of evil. It may be that they do, but if so it is not so much in the giving of committed teaching to this effect as in the offering of gentle hints. We need to be cautious before we are able to ground a doctrine of the fall of angels on uncertain exegesis. There is considerable wisdom in retreating into agnosticism, with Emil Brunner, at this point. Yet it is significant that Brunner, while dismissing the doctrine, nevertheless goes on to speak of Satan as the point of origin and self-generation of evil.[28] The point is that whatever obscurity may surround the biblical texts, there are good *theological* reasons for moving towards the concept of an angelic fall.

The value of the concept of the angelic catastrophe is that it locates the origin of evil within the created sphere. Evil comes from a deliberate misuse of creaturely freedom initially on a transcendent, spiritual level and then on the human plane. We may agree with Barth that evil has no honourable ontological status. But it does have an ontological *ground* in the freedom of men and of angels.[29] It may be parasitical, but it is not passive. It is forceful and dynamic in its own negative way. To speak in terms of a 'fall of angels' may appear to be a somewhat mythological way of speaking of such an event. But there is in fact no analytical way in which it is possible to speak of events and realities in this spiritual, pre-human and transcendent realm. Pictorial though the language may be, it is the nearest and most accurate formulation we are likely to discover.

That evil has its origin in the created sphere is implied by Colossians 1:16, which understands Christ as the origin of both visible and invisible realities, and by Romans 8:28–39 which brackets the principalities and powers which might seek to separate us from the love of God among created things. Evil is not therefore an inevitable part of the structure of things but an aberration and a rebellion of an inexcusable kind within the creation.

Barth denied the possibility of such a fall on the basis of his angelology. To admit the possibility of such an event denies the concept of angels he has articulated. His understanding of angels is immensely valuable and rings true with the marginal and mysterious role angels play in Scripture. But he has no substantial biblical grounds for depriving angels of the kind of being and freedom which would make it possible for them to rebel. It is possible to conceive of angelic powers having their own way of being and some degree of autonomy, sufficient for there to have been an aberration. It is possible at this point to agree with Barth that such an act would deprive angelic powers of their true existence and would cause them to exist only in a negative and chaotic form, feeding parasitically on the good and ordered creation. The concept of nothingness expresses well what an angelic power might become once it departed from obedience to God. It would exist in contradiction to God, deprived of validity, existing as a negative and malevolent spiritual agency wholly given over to evil and to the thwarting of God's purpose. Barth himself suggests as much when he says that an angel which behaved unangelically would resemble a demon:

> Although he is a creature, and an exemplary and perfect creature, his task as such has simply been to come and then to go again, to pass by. He would be a lying spirit, a demon, if he were to tarry, directing attention and love and honour and even perhaps adoration for himself and enticing man to enter into dealings and fellowship with himself instead of through him into dealings with God.[30]

A further weakness of Barth's view is that it is difficult for it to explain the biblical understanding of an evil *strategy* which recognises some degree of deliberate, malevolent *purpose* within the power of darkness.[31] The concept of the angelic fall would make this intelligible since it identifies the factor of intelligence in this evil power. As to whether or not angels have it within their being to disobey God and fall, we maintain, in disagreement with Barth, that this must be seen as a real possibility.

7. Step seven

To argue as I have done does not in any way explain evil. To say that there is such an origin for evil may expound and describe the point of origin but it does not explain how and why it is that an angelic rebellion, or whatever is referred to by such pictorial language, should take place. We are here posed with a genuine difficulty. Even accepting that there is a freedom of angelic beings to rebel against God, we have no explanation as to why they should wish to do this. We may assert that such a freedom introduces into the creation a riskiness that God has actually built into the world he has made. But this does not explain where the impulse to misuse such freedom has come from. Wink's suggestion that Satan (or should we say Lucifer?) in his proper mode of being was to fulfil the task of proving and testing humanity by representing the choices that were alternatives to God's will and that his fall came when he overstepped the mark in his role of agent provocateur, is an intriguing one. Of course Wink is only speaking of this as a symbol of something which actually happened in humanity, but taken more literally it still has a validity. Satan's fall would be seen as going too far in a direction in which he was already set. The impulse to overstep the mark becomes more comprehensible on this understanding. However, as the Bible supplies us with too little to speak with authority in this realm, we do well to maintain a silence.

There is another reason why it might be reasonable of us to feel that at this point we have reached the limits of our knowledge. There is a fundamental sense in which evil is not something that can be made sense of. The essence of evil is that it is something which is absurd, bizarre and irrational. It is the nature of evil to be inexplicable, an enigma and a stupidity. Therefore there can be no explanation of its origin. Indeed, to answer the question as to why evil exists and to incorporate it into a rational system which 'makes sense' of it is a dangerous thing to do. Once we acknowledge that it has a reason for its existence we are beginning to make evil relatively good. We are saying that it is not as evil as it seems. Evil therefore ceases to be evil and we lose the sense of horror and abhorrence which is the only attitude which we should rightly entertain towards it. The true nature of evil is revealed at the cross where the unholy conspiracy of world, flesh and devil, crucify the Son of God in violent and total violation of all possible laws of love, humanity and decency. Here evil was shown up in its true nature and there is nothing good that can be said of it, and no good thought that could be entertained now or ever. Because evil is absurd and irrational in its very nature, we have reached the limit of what may be said in rational language.

8. Step eight

While being critical of the concept of nothingness, it does illuminate us in a further step. Evil is inexplicable and yet the possibility of it exists as the negative side of a positive world. It exists by mimicry, contradiction and distortion. It can only exist as a process of discreativity dependent on God's creativity. Evil is self-generating but it is not, strictly speaking, self-creating. The power of darkness is not able to create anything. It can only distort what already exists. As C. S. Lewis has it:

> Goodness is, so to speak, itself: badness is only spoiled goodness. And there must be something good before it can be spoiled... evil is a parasite, not an original thing.[32]

67

The possibility of evil exists however by virtue of God's creative work, but only as its reverse side and denial, as that which God excludes from his own work. Evil functions as a form of anti-matter, a kind of cosmic black hole which wars against that which is created and sustained by God and yet can only exist by virtue of it. God has created a world in which this possibility exists of necessity. Barth is correct in saying that God's creative Yes! implies a No!. Where he is wrong is in saying that God's implied No! actually gives rise to evil. The fact of a possibility does not create a reality corresponding to it, but it does allow the possibility that malevolence will arise within creation and give actuality to the possibility of evil. This malevolent power is the devil who himself was a creature of God but who through his aberration and rebellion has forfeited his proper being, exists solely as a negative power without a future and being spirit has become totally and irredeemably evil, a manifestation of pure wickedness.

9. Step nine

God in creating this world made it with the possibility that it might go astray inherent within it. This implies that he has built into it a certain freedom over against himself and that this freedom is of the essence of what it means for humans to be human and for the world to be the world. Because this was God's intention and the fact of evil cannot have been unforeseen and must therefore have been permitted by him, it must also follow that God is not without responsibility. He is not the author of evil, but he is the author of creation and of the risk inherent in it. As we will see, the significance of the cross of Jesus is that the one who suffers most because of sin is not mankind but God himself and it is by his own action in the cross that the power of evil is actually overcome. At the cross, Jesus

Christ broke the power of the devil. This victory comes from God alone.[33]

10. Step ten

The fact that on the cross evil was overcome does not mean that the conflict with the powers of darkness does not continue. There is a fierce conflict yet to be waged and the worst of the conflict may yet be to come. Nevertheless, the decisive victory which has already been achieved awaits its fulfilment and consummation. Many years ago, Oscar Cullmann applied to this the analogy of D-Day and V-Day. When the allied forces, in the struggle to liberate occupied Europe landed on the Normandy beaches, they won the decisive victory. From that point on the result of the war was a foregone conclusion. Yet it was some time before victory was finally proclaimed in Europe. In the intervening period the battle was at its fiercest as a cornered enemy fought to the bitter end. So, Cullmann wrote:

> In the time between the resurrection and the Parousia of Christ [the angelic powers] are, so to speak, bound as to a rope which can be more or less lengthened, so that those among them who show tendencies to emancipation can have the illusion that they are releasing themselves from their bond with Christ, while in reality, by this striving which here and there appears, they only show once more their original demonic character; they cannot, however, actually set themselves free. Their power is only apparent. The church has so much more the duty to stand against them, in view of the fact that it knows that their power is only apparent and that in reality Christ has already conquered all demons.[34]

Earlier on we were at pains to stress the irrationality of

evil, our inability to fit it neatly into a system that makes sense. We stand by that. But now we are also able to assert that because God is the Lord of heaven and earth he is able to make even this senseless and meaningless evil serve his own purpose. This is not because evil has its own hidden meaning but because against its own will, God is able to make it serve a greater meaning. The cross is the supreme example of how God is able to master evil and cause even that to serve his good purpose.

Having attempted to capture something of the essence and the form of evil our attention will now turn to what is commonly called 'the problem of evil'.

REFERENCES

1. Emil Brunner *The Christian Doctrine of Creation and Redemption* (London, 1952) pp107–108.
2. Rom 6:12–23.
3. Rom 7:5–11.
4. Eph 6:12.
5. D. E. H. Whiteley *The Theology of St Paul* (Oxford, 1972) p19.
6. Wesley Carr *Angels and Principalities* (Cambridge, 1981) pp175–6.
7. J. R. W. Stott *God's New Society* (Leicester, 1979) pp267–275.
8. Eg 1 Cor 2:8; Tit 3:1; Rom 8:38. See Michael Green *I Believe in Satan's Downfall* (London, 1981) pp81–86.
9. Hendrik Berkhof *The Christian Faith* (Grand Rapids, 1979) pp208–209.
10. Col 1:16.
11. A. B. Come *An Introduction to Barth's Dogmatics for Preachers* (London, 1963) p220.
12. John Macquarrie *Principles of Christian Theology* (London, 1966) p241.
13. Paul Tillich *Systematic Theology* Vol III (London, 1968) pp108–109.
14. 1 Jn 3:8; Lk 10:18. See also J. D. G. Dunn and Graham H. Twelftree 'Demon Possession and Exorcism in the NT' *Churchman* **94** No 3 (1980) pp222–3.
15. See Helmut Thielicke *The Evangelical Faith* Vol III (Grand Rapids, 1982) p451.
16. Brunner *op cit* p139.

17. Wolf Kroetke *Suende und Nichtiges bei Karl Barth* (Berlin, 1983) p27.
18. C. S. Lewis *Mere Christianity* (London, 1952) p44.
19. Eg Ex 4:21, 18; 15; Rom 9:17; 1 Sam 16:14; Mt 18:7.
20. John Calvin *Institutes* III, xxiii, 8.
21. Brunner *op cit* p139.
22. See the previous chapter.
23. Eg CD II/2 pp122–124.
24. Brunner *op cit* pp133–137.
25. Michael Green *op cit* pp33–42 makes far too much of these verses.
26. See on this Walther Eichrodt *Ezekiel* (London, 1970) p392; John Mauchline *Isaiah 1–39* (London, 1962) p140.
27. J. N. D. Kelly *The Epistles of Peter and of Jude* (London, 1969) p331.
28. Brunner *op cit* p139.
29. Donald Bloesch *Jesus is Victor! Karl Barth's Doctrine of Salvation* (Nashville, 1976) p170.
30. CD III/3 p481.
31. Eg Mt 13:39; Eph 6:11; 1 Pet 5:8; Rev 20:2.
32. C. S. Lewis *Mere Christianity* pp46–47.
33. Jn 12:31–33; Col 1:19–20, 2:15; 1 Jn 3:8.
34. Oscar Cullmann *Christ and Time* (London, 1951) p198.

CHAPTER FIVE

The Problem of Evil

No greater challenge is posed to Christian belief than that which is normally called 'the problem of evil'. This is true on both the philosophical and personal levels. There are few of us who pass through life unscathed. Most of us experience at one time or another the way in which life can deal the cruellest of blows through a painful illness, a sudden death, a tragic accident. At such times it is not unusual for us to ask the questions, why does God allow this? If he is so loving and so powerful, why does he not interfere and stop it? Why did he allow it in the first place? How can a Father deal with his children in this way? People will often excuse themselves from actively believing in God on the basis that they have 'seen too much in life'. What they are saying is that a simple, hopeful belief in a loving God seems too naive a faith in such a complex world.

Those who find such a faith difficult may of course simply be using the world's suffering as an excuse for avoiding God. But it would be an insensitive person or a stupid one who did not feel themselves questioning when faced with blatant and senseless suffering. In the twentieth century we perhaps know more of this than our forefathers, not only because we are better informed about what is going on in the world but also because we have seen a vast amount of inhumanity in our own century. The horrendous slaughter of the Great War and the senseless squandering of human lives for the sake of the balance of power exploded the optimistic hopes for the perfecting of the human race held by previous generations. The death camps of the Second World War, the nuclear devastation of Hiroshima and Nagasaki, the fire-storms of Hamburg and Dresden, to say nothing of the countless smaller wars and acts of atrocity which have continued unabated ever since, may very well cause us to ask whether the God of the universe is a loving Father or a cosmic sadist.

Nowhere is this question put more movingly or with greater moral authority than in the writings of the 1986 Nobel Prize winner, Eli Wiesel. In his book *Night*, Wiesel records his teenage years spent in the concentration camps at Auschwitz and Buchenwald. The book is dedicated to his parents and his little sister, Tzapora. He had seen his mother, sister and all his family disappear into the ovens. His father was to die more slowly. The story is told with infinitely deep sadness. From his earliest days as the child of a devout Jewish family, Wiesel had loved God with a profound and rare instinct. But for this child, the concentration camp was to destroy the God he had known.

Never shall I forget that night, the first night in the camp, which has turned my life into one long night, seven times cursed and seven times sealed. Never shall I forget that smoke. Never shall I forget the little faces of the children, whose bodies I saw turned into wreaths of smoke beneath a silent blue sky. Never shall I forget those flames which consumed my faith for ever. Never shall I forget that nocturnal silence which deprived me, for all eternity, of the desire to live. Never shall I forget those moments which murdered my God and my soul and turned my dreams to dust. Never shall I forget these things, even if I am condemned to live as long as God Himself. Never.[1]

In another place he describes an experience which must have been shared by thousands:

Once, New Year's Day had dominated my life. I knew that my sins grieved the Eternal; I implored his forgiveness. Once, I had believed profoundly that upon one solitary deed of mine, one solitary prayer, depended the salvation of the world. This day I had ceased to plead. I was no longer capable of lamentation. On the contrary, I felt very strong. I was the accuser, God the accused. My eyes were open and I was alone — terribly alone in a world without God and without man, without love or mercy. I had ceased to be anything but ashes, yet I felt myself to be stronger than the Almighty, to whom my life had been tied for so long. I stood amid that praying congregation, observing it like a stranger.[2]

Who among us is able to dismiss such experience or such questions as trivial? It must be that the Christian belief in God has something to say. Perhaps at the end of the chapter we may have something to say, but any answer must be hard won, for it cannot be lightly given.

The personal experience of suffering gives rise to the philosophical question concerning the existence of God. The argument against the existence of God was cogently stated by the eighteenth century English philosopher David Hume:

Is he willing to prevent evil, but not able? then he is impotent. Is he able, but not willing? then he is malevolent. Is he both able and willing? whence then is evil?[3]

The problem is posed here in terms of a logical dilemma which calls the existence of God into question. The bulk of this chapter will be concerned with a response to this dilemma and towards the conclusion of the chapter we will return to the personal dimensions of the issue.

Before reviewing various responses to the question posed by Hume it will be helpful to outline several distinctions in the form which evil takes. There is first of all *metaphysical evil*. By this we mean that form of evil which transcends individual human minds and causes us to look for a trans-human source. In the previous two chapters our attention has been largely given to this dimension.[4] A second form of evil is that of *moral evil*, that is, evil which can be attributed to the misuse of mankind's own moral freedom. A third form is that of *physical* or *passive evil* by which is meant those forms of suffering and destruction which are to be found in the physical universe and cannot be directly attributed to mankind's sinful behaviour. Moral and physical evil will be the kinds of evil which will occupy our attention in this chapter, although there will be some attempt to explore the relations between them and metaphysical evil.

1. Responses to the problem of evil

How then have thinkers responded to the dilemma posed by the problem of evil? A variety of possible positions is here set out.

(a) Evil as illusion. One way of escaping from the dilemma is to deny the existence of evil and to argue that it is an illusion. This is characteristic of Hindu religion which affirms that ultimate reality is both one and good and therefore that which appears in this world to be many and evil is actually illusion. This 'monism' (understanding the world in terms of one single ground or cause) has no room for any kind of dualism (the belief that two opposing principles are at work). A modern form of this kind of belief in the West is Christian Science which understands evil as a false perception, an error of the mortal mind. Sin, sickness and death do not exist in reality.

The questions posed by this attitude are considerable. Why does the illusion appear so real if it does not exist? And if the illusion feels so real, what practical difference does it make to view it as an illusion? Or to quote Edward Lear:

> A certain faith-healer of Deal
> Asserted: 'Pain is not real!'
> 'Then pray tell me why',
> Came the patient's reply,
> 'When I sit on a pin
> And puncture my skin,
> Do I hate what I fancy I feel?'[5]

The concept of illusion does not help to resolve the problem of evil since it raises too many questions about itself.

(b) God as finite. A second approach to the dilemma is to alter the premises on which the argument is based. If God is good, but not almighty, then we have an adequate explanation of why he does not deal with evil. He does not because he cannot. God also is the victim of evil in the world, as are we. This of course is the solution posed by dualism. God's power is not absolute and therefore he is not in full control of evil. He too is struggling against it. A view which is similar in this respect is represented by *process theology*, certain versions of which (not all) view God as finite and limited. Process theology sees reality not as a series of static objects but as a process of becoming. God is in the world luring it towards harmony and the good. Evil consists of incompatible factors which need to be accepted and then transformed into the process which moves towards the good. God is involved in the process of struggling with evil and mankind is called to co-operate with God in this struggle upwards and forwards.

Some aspects of this way of thinking are of considerable value but grave problems are caused by the concept of a finite God and by the view that God can absorb evil into himself in his ongoing process of becoming. It is difficult to see how these themes in process thought can be squared with biblical faith.

(c) Evil as good. A third response to the problem of evil will be exposed to the same kind of criticism we have just made of process theology. This approach seeks to deny the absolutely evil nature of evil and argues that it is really a disguised form of the good. It will prove necessary to spend some time on this response since the issues it raises are complex and our discussion of it will not be exhausted in this section.

The creative voice in this context belongs to the philosopher Gottfried von Leibnitz (1646–1716) who sought to refute the argument from evil by maintaining that this is the best of all possible worlds. The world is moving towards perfection. It is not yet perfect but in achieving perfection, the evil aspects of it are essential ingredients in the whole.[6] The conclusion to be drawn from this is that evil cannot really be regarded as evil since it is actually serving a good purpose. It is the means of moral growth through which perfection is being achieved and therefore even the pain of life can be seen to serve a good purpose.

It will be recognised that this is similar to process theology in its perception that evil which is accepted and built upon may actually be the means of progress towards the good. The fact that good has its opposite in evil actually serves to enhance the good, to show it up by contrast and to bring out its true goodness. It may be seen how this operates in our own lives. There are many unpleasant and difficult experiences which we would not choose to undergo but which are thrust upon us so that we have no choice. These trials are difficult at the time but it is through them that we actually grow in character. Suffering does sometimes produce growth in human development when it is accepted without bitterness and yielded up to God. Looking back we may say about many such experiences that we have actually benefited from them, we are better people as a result. Furthermore, this appears to be confirmed by Scripture which speaks of God's painful discipline that later 'produces a harvest of righteousness and peace for those who have been trained by it'[7] and affirms that 'in all things God works for the good of those who love him'.[8] Perhaps, after all, evil is not really all that evil but simply a disguised form of the good!

A significant contribution to this discussion has been made by John A. Sanford, an Episcopalian priest and psychoanalyst.[9] Sanford seeks to develop insights from the works of the pioneering psychologist Carl Gustav Jung and argues that to understand evil helps us better to understand God.[10] Evil has therefore a very positive role to play in the development of individuals. It is the shadow side of reality which belongs as of right to creation and just as the person without a shadow does not exist physically so we cannot exist as true persons without a shadow. Sanford argues that what we judge evil depends on the perspective from which we speak. Only the ultimate, divine perspective would enable us to see the positive role of evil within universal human history.[11] Specifically, evil helps the development of human nature by stimulating its capacity for moral feeling. It acts as a catalyst in enabling growth towards individual wholeness. The shadow is therefore necessary for the growth of the human personality.[12] Far from being wholly evil it is, like Mephistopheles in Goethe's Faust, 'part of that force which would do evil yet forever works the good'.[13]

There is considerable force to this argument and much that is attractive. There are echoes here of Walter Wink's concept of the devil as God's servant, his 'holy sifter'. Yet caution needs to be exercised before we go too far too fast down this road. Sanford himself, in expounding the thought of Jung, sees the danger of this tendency. Jung criticised the traditional concept of evil because it belittled evil and thereby, in his opinion, belittled the good.

> There is no white without black, no right without left, no above without below, no warm without cold, no truth without error, no light without darkness etc. If Evil is an illusion God is necessarily illusory too.[14]

Such thinking causes Jung to argue that evil must not only be necessary for man but also for God. The Christian doctrine of God lacks, he considers, the necessary dimension of a dark side. In place of the doctrine of the Trinity he advocates the concept of Quaternity, in which the Adversary takes his place along with Father, Son and Spirit within the Godhead.[15]

What is happening here? First of all, evil has been declared to be no longer truly evil. Secondly, the idea of an ultimate and radical hostility between God and evil has been lost sight of. Thirdly, the devil has been enthroned within the Godhead as a divine person. There is a logical progression to this which means that once the irreducible and unqualified wickedness of evil has been lost sight of, it is not long before the devil takes his place and reigns in divine splendour. As we shall see, the concept of the shadow side has something to commend it, but it is not along the lines suggested by Jung. Evil cannot be seen as part of the good or even as necessary to it since to do that is to make evil itself partly good.

(d) Evil as necessary. At this point we turn to our final possible response to the problem of evil, the view that evil is the product of the misuse of God-given freedom and that the possibility that free beings might choose evil rather than good is a necessary part of human freedom. This position is known as the 'free-will defence'. It counters Hume's objection that God cannot be both omnipotent and loving in view of the fact of evil by seeing it as an oversimplification of the actual case. God is both omnipotent and loving and as such has created mankind as free beings. As it is logically impossible for God to create a free being who automatically does what is right (in this case there would be no freedom) he has therefore introduced into the creation a freedom which is neither conditioned nor predetermined. Mankind has relative freedom over God and is therefore able to disobey and resist him. This does not compromise the omnipotence of God since this does not mean that God can do that which is logically impossible. He cannot create a square circle or a colour which is simultaneously black and white. These are logical impossibilities and so is the idea of a free being who automatically chooses the right. God might have chosen not to create a world at all, or a world populated by sinless robots. Actually he has chosen to create a world in which there are free creatures because it is the best possible way towards the kind of world and the kind of people God ultimately desires. This is not inconsistent with the love of

God because the love of God is demonstrated in the very freedom which he gives to humans. Yet such freedom carries with it great risks and it is the riskiness of love which means that there is suffering in the world. The free-will defence therefore maintains that God is omnipotent, omniscient and wholly good but that it was not within God's power to create a world containing moral good without creating one containing the possibility of moral evil.[16] The risk of evil is therefore a necessary part of free existence and is incompatible with neither the power nor the love of God.

The last paragraph has approached the problem of evil as a logical problem. Yet this is not the only way to do this. Much disbelief in God today is not so much scientifically calculated rejection of the proposition 'God exists' as a heartfelt protest against the depth and extent of human suffering. This 'protest atheism' rejects the existence of a loving God because the notion seems implausible in the light of the facts. It is not enough to demonstrate, therefore, the possibility of moral evil as necessarily involved in human freedom. When we are actually faced with human suffering, logical arguments are somewhat hollow. What the Christian faith offers is the belief, not yet provable, that there is 'a future good great enough to justify all that has happened on the way to it'.[17] It must be said that in view of the amount of suffering this future would have to be great indeed to outweigh it. But it is just this vision of the future which the Bible offers us when it speaks of a restored and healed world in which suffering and sorrow have no place.[18] The model for this confidence is the cross of Christ which is simultaneously the focus of the worst evil and the greatest good. The powers of darkness beyond and within the human race do their worst and seek to obliterate the man of supreme goodness in a horrific way. The Christ suffers and is rejected. Yet this event is also the greatest revelation of the love of God who by enduring evil in Christ actually overcomes it. It is because of this that Christians are able to believe that all things can be seen to fulfil the purpose of God. Evil is not of God and is in no sense good, but God's power is such that even evil can be made ultimately to serve him.[19] God is the God who creates out of nothing. This does not make evil less evil and should not lead us to entertain positive ideas about it, but it is a testimony to the power of God who is able to bring good out of evil just as he was able to create the world out of nothing.

A recent TV advertisement for the *Guardian* newspaper may help to understand this. It showed the same scene from three different angles. In the first shot a young man is dressed as a skinhead and runs towards a well dressed businessman carrying a briefcase, knocking him over. The conclusion the viewer draws is that the skinhead is mugging the businessman with the intention of robbing him. In the second shot the scene is shown from a different angle. This time it is seen that behind the skinhead a car has drawn up and three beefy looking men climb out. The skinhead runs towards the businessman and knocks him over. The viewer revises his interpretation and concludes that the skinhead is being chased by plain clothes policemen and in his flight accidentally sends the businessman sprawling. The third shot is taken from above and this time it can be seen that above the businessman a load is suspended from a crane. It is about to slip and to fall on top of the man. What is actually happening is that the skinhead has seen the danger and is running towards the man to push him out of the way and so save his life at the risk of his own. At the end of the advert the message is that the *Guardian* gives the right perspective on things and the viewer is left repenting of his or her prejudices!

To understand events correctly we need to have the right

perspective on them. We do not yet have that perspective because we are too close to the action. As time passes we gain greater perspective on events. But it is only in the light of the fullness of time that we are able to understand both the meaning of events and the role they have played in the purpose of God. In the light of God's ultimate purpose it will be seen that evil, though immense, is finite, while the good for which God is preparing us is infinite. The ultimate joy will therefore greatly surpass the present sorrow and suffering in the created order. It is with this faith and hope that Christians live in the present, believing that as God worked through the events of the cross to achieve the reconciliation of mankind to himself so he is working through the events of history towards his final goal of the reconciliation of all things.

2. The problem of physical evil

We have not as yet exhausted the problem of evil. We have so far in this book given an account of metaphysical and moral evil, but what about physical evil? It has often been remarked that as Freud took the lid off human consciousness and revealed the mass of conflicting drives and emotions in human beings, so Darwin before him took the lid off nature and demonstrated how it was 'red in tooth and claw'. Suffering is not confined to the human species. The animal creation is aware of pain. It is expressed in the way in which one species preys upon another and death and dying are a part of the cycle of creation. Conflict appears to be a normative part of the animal kingdom. Then there are natural disasters, earthquakes, floods, volcanoes, hurricanes, which cannot be attributed to the moral choices of people in any direct sense. Physical evil poses the question about the nature of the Creator God. If the creation reflects the being of God its Creator, then surely the Creator too must have his dark side, a cruel, sadistic streak? How may Christians respond to evil at this level? Once more we survey a number of responses.

(a) The problem is not as bad as it seems. This response argues that it is possible to exaggerate the problem of pain in relation to the physical universe. The animal kingdom is characterized by co-operation far more than conflict and it is possible to give many examples of different species living and functioning harmoniously together. The conflict that does exist serves a useful purpose in that predatory behaviour is necessary to prevent decrepit old age or decomposing carcases. The life of many animals may be short and threatened, but they exist without the kind of anxiety that humans know. Animal pain is real but is not as bad as human beings may imagine. Their nervous systems are less developed than ours and provide a possible anaesthetic when wounded. We need to beware of the 'pathetic fallacy' which imagines that animals have a human consciousness of their own existence. In fact their manner of existence is different from ours. They have great enjoyment in their existence. Besides, at lower levels of animal life and in the vegetable kingdom, to talk of evil in the way we do becomes meaningless. The problem of physical pain is therefore by no means as great as may be imagined. Even then it must be recognised that pain fulfils a useful purpose. It acts as a warning signal and, indeed, actually highlights the joy of existing.

This reductionist approach to physical evil certainly encourages us to put things in perspective. It can however be objected that in the animal world (and in human beings taken as animals) there are elements which do not easily find explanation. For instance, the onset of cancer is not accompanied by pain as a warning that something is wrong. The process is the other way round in that cancer begins painlessly and becomes progressively more painful. Such pain serves no useful purpose whatever and it is this meaningless element that is problematic. Despite these elements it can be argued quite cogently that the nature of much created life is transient. The physical world exists in a process of change where all the units of nature are in flux.

> The ongoing life of nature flows, so to speak, through these units, and each of them has its own brief period of individual existence before the elements composing it are reclaimed, only to be organised again into new forms within the larger whole.[20]

This account of the nature of the creation leaves us with a world in which there are co-operation and conflict and which is therefore both impressive and fierce. Yet such a world is clean and noble in its own way with the conflict fulfilling a higher purpose in which the life of each unit is yielded up into the greater whole. The difficulty comes in accounting for the forms of pain which cannot be made to fit into this scheme and are seemingly without meaning.

(b) Physical evil is the result of mankind's moral evil. Another attempt to account for physical evil attributes it directly or indirectly to mankind's sin. This is plainly true in the disruptive effect that man can have upon the environment. The callous disregard for creation which often accompanies mankind's desire to exploit the world's resources is certainly an increasingly significant factor in an industrialised world. It is even true that disease is to an extent the result of mankind's choice to live in certain ways. We are intimately linked to our environment. But traditional accounts of the fall of man have sometimes pointed to the fact that mankind was created as the viceregent of creation. The command was given to rule over the earth.[21] Mankind was the high point of creation with all things placed under them.[22] The fall resulting from rebellion against God means that this position has been lost. Instead of ruling mankind is now alienated from the Creator and the creation. Instead of existing in harmony with it, the Creation is now hostile. The ground is cursed and brings forth thorns and thistles.[23]

It is argued that the fall of the human race leads to a fall of creation because the whole of creation is bound up with human rulership of it. The physical evil which we see in creation does not properly belong to the creation but is there because in its fall mankind has taken the creation with it. According to Calvin, Adam by his original sin 'perverted the whole order of nature in heaven and on earth'.[24] The conflict, cruelty and pain in creation must therefore be attributed directly to human sin. In support of this view, a number of significant biblical details may be mustered.

(i) There is the testimony of Genesis 1–3 which clearly portrays the creation of a good world. Genesis 1 gives an account of seven days in which God creates the world, pronouncing over it at the end of each stage that it is good. When the work is completed with the creation of humanity he pronounces it 'very good'[25] and he and the creation enter into a sabbath rest of blessedness. This idyllic scene is disrupted by the rebellion and disobedience at which point mankind and creation go wrong.

The theodicy of Christian theology, building upon the scriptural testimony defends the goodness of God by setting the free decision of the first man as the factor 'bringing death into the world and all our woe'.[26]

The Fair Face of Evil

(ii) A second detail is that of Paul's teaching concerning the first Adam in Romans 5:12–14 which would appear to confirm the picture presented under (i). Here, according to Paul, sin and its companion death, have entered the world through Adam's sin. It is concluded therefore that the creation prior to Adam was free from death.

(iii) There appears to be further confirmation in Romans 8:20 which speaks of the creation being 'subjected to frustration, not by its own choice, but by the will of the one who subjected it'. By this subjection, creation has entered into a 'bondage to decay'. Understood within the context of the two previous points, it is possible to take this to mean that through the sin of man the world has become subject to death and to the cycle of decay. Although the one who subjects the world to frustration is usually considered to be God himself, it is in view of the sin of man that this subjection takes place.

According to this view, then, physical evil is directly attributable to moral evil and God himself is cleared of responsibility. But there are problems. The chief among them is the problem posed by the theory of evolution. An evolutionary understanding of human development would hold that, far from death and decay entering into the physical world through Adam's sin, they are inherent in nature itself, functioning as an essential part of the evolutionary process. Furthermore, evolutionists would argue that the evidence for pain and suffering in the animal kingdom prior to the appearance of mankind on earth is unambiguously clear in the fossil records. To maintain this particular interpretation of Scripture it would therefore be necessary to construct an alternative scientific model which would be in harmony with the biblical interpretation. This has not been convincingly achieved, despite the loud protestations of the creationist lobby to the contrary.

Further difficulties attend this view. A world which is totally free of death and decay is one which would be radically different from the world we presently know. These processes are an absolutely essential part of the existence and maintenance of the world we know such that a world constructed on a different pattern ceases to bear any resemblance to a world in which, for instance, the seasonal cycle of growth, death and decay is not only fundamental but also in its own way beautiful. Indeed, the Genesis record does not suggest a world that is perfect and not prone to decay. Adam and Eve are placed in the garden to subdue and manage it, presumably because it had the capacity to get out of hand. Furthermore, the significant detail of Genesis 3:22 where God is said to guard against their eating of the tree of life, suggests that Adam and Eve were not inherently immortal. Immortality was a possibility open to them rather than an inherent quality. If this be so about mankind it becomes necessary to think about the animal kingdom as prone to death and dying. In fact, this interpretation is quite consistent with both Genesis 3:3 and Romans 5:12 where it is the death of men and women which are the result of sin, not the entry of death and decay into the physical world. It seems far more likely that death and decay are actually part of the processes of the good creation. Everyone's body can be understood as being subject to death in the physical sense yet with the opportunity through maintaining fellowship with God of entering into immortality. In this case the death that enters through sin is not physical cessation of existence but the death in alienation and anxiety which is characteristic of humanity out of fellowship with God. Were men and women not sinners, their physical life might well have come to its natural end, but not in death as we now know it but in a transition to glory such as that apparently experienced by Enoch.[27]

In the light of these difficulties, there is a variant of the view that Adam's sin is the cause of the fall of the physical universe. This is the view that the fall of Adam not only affected creation prospectively in the sense that a transition from an original to an imperfect creation took place in time through Adam's sin, but also affected creation retrospectively. The fall of Adam may therefore be regarded as the cause of the frustrated nature of creation both before and after the actual time of Adam's sin.[28] This view is represented by Bruce Milne who sees a link between sin and suffering in that:

> all our sinning flows from Adam's primal act of folly which subjected the whole universe prospectively and retrospectively to the forces of decay and cosmic wickedness, and hence to the possibility of suffering and tragedy.[29]

This is a somewhat more subtle approach to the issue which argues that Romans 8:20, which speaks of the subjection of the creation to frustration presumably by God, does not specify when this took place. It could therefore be the case that as it was God who subjected the world, he did this prior to Adam's existence but nevertheless in view of the forthcoming sin which he foresaw. What happens in sequence with mankind may be deemed to happen simultaneously to the eternal God and therefore, viewed from God's point of view there need be no sequential fall of creation, but nevertheless one which is consequent upon mankind's foreseen sin.

(c) Physical evil is caused by the devil's fall, not man's. A major difficulty with the preceding view consists in the fact that, according to Genesis 3, there was already, before mankind came into existence, an element in the creation which was fallen. This is represented in Eden by the snake which tempted and misled Adam and Eve. Here we have an indication that human sin, potent though it may be, nevertheless needs to be understood within the wider context of a power working in opposition to God. Here we return to the notion of metaphysical evil, the idea that there was an aberration in creation prior to the fall of mankind. We have already discussed this in terms of a 'fall of angels', that is, a rebellion against God of spiritual beings created by him. To do this in the light of the free-will defence we need to assert that such creatures, like humans, are free. If this is accepted it becomes possible to think in terms of physical evil being the result of the activity of such powers within creation prior to the appearance of human beings. Natural evil may be attributed to the free action of non-human persons. In favour of this point of view it may be noted that on one occasion at least Jesus attributed disease directly to Satan and recognised his agency in this regard.[30]

A modern representative of this point of view is C. S. Lewis who argued that as it is no longer possible to trace animal suffering to the fall of Adam, it could be attributed to a Satanic corruption, but he limits this to the animal sphere. The vegetable kingdom may also exhibit the tendency for plant to prey on plant but this he does not consider as evil. Yet in the animal kingdom this tendency is intrinsically evil. Just as the fall of man involves his fall back into animality, so a similar Satanic corruption in the animal world involves their slipping back into behaviour proper to vegetables.[31] Animal pain is not God's handiwork but is begun by Satan's malice and perpetuated by man's desertion of his post. Lewis ventures the speculation that man at his first coming into the world may already have had a redemptive function to perform, sharing in the rescue of creation from the corruption of Satan.[32]

What is remarkable about this view is that although it is valid in its own terms and may be correct, there is little that would specifically support it in Scripture. The fall of angels is only lightly represented and there is nothing that may be held to shed light upon the involvement of the power of darkness in the animal order.

(d) Physical evil and the shadow across creation. The fourth possible response to the question of physical evil which will be discussed here is the one with which the author feels most comfortable. It is the view that the majority of what is called 'physical evil' is misnamed and that the creation as it is, apart from the moral evil which may be attributed to mankind and possibly to the devil, is substantially, although not entirely, as God intended it. This approach therefore while believing in the fall of man, does not accept that it precipitated the creation into a fallen state but that the creation was already acquainted with the kinds of conflicts which we are here discussing.

To develop this point of view, we need to return to the concept of the 'Shadow' of which C. G. Jung speaks. The way in which this concept is expounded by Jung led to the enthronement of Satan as a member of the Godhead. This we rejected as a fatal mistake. Yet the idea that there is a shadow side to creation has been advanced by Karl Barth in a way which completely avoids this error by distinguishing radically between 'the Shadow' and 'nothingness', that is to say, evil. By the Shadow[33] Barth means that creation and existence involve both negative and positive aspects. The negative aspects are not to be identified with evil but rather are to be seen as parts of God's good creation. The Shadow includes: 'hours, days and years both bright and dark, success and failure, laughter and tears, growth and age, gain and loss, birth and sooner or later its inevitable corollary, death'.[34] What he here indicates is the fact that creation has its threatening side and that this is not in itself evil. Mankind was not placed into a world where he would be cushioned from discomfort, struggle and effort, failure or disappointment but into a world where through the struggle of earthly existence they would undergo a soul-making experience whereby through difficulty and demand they would grow to maturity. The Shadow therefore exists in creation not as something evil in itself but as that which would cause mankind to depend upon God for help and strength. This shadow does not jeopardize the nature of the creation as good since God's judgement in Genesis 1:31 does not imply that the creation was perfect and without what we would consider to be negative aspects. Rather, the goodness of creation consists in its being suitable for God's purposes and for mankind within them.[35] It is an appropriate sphere for mankind to learn to enter into relationship with God. According to Barth, creaturely being contains two aspects, a Yes and a No, joy and misery, but both have their foundation in the will of God and are reflections of the majesty and lowliness of God himself.[36]

On the face of it it may appear that Barth is saying what we have already rejected, namely that evil is really good. The crucial point to note is that he makes a clear distinction between the Shadow and evil. The Shadow is dark, but this does not mean it is evil. It belongs to that category of events and experiences which seem to us at the time to be difficult, but for which we are grateful in due course because we recognise that we have benefited through them. Evil, on the other hand, is not of this character. It is utterly evil and is not created by God. The point is that *evil uses the Shadow as an alibi.*[37] It hides behind it and seeks to persuade people that it is identical with it. The result is that we run two dangers. On the one hand we may call evil good because we confuse it with the Shadow (as did

Jung). On the other hand, for the same reason we may
end up calling the Shadow evil. We need therefore to
distinguish between the two quite clearly. There are difficult experiences in life which belong to the Shadow and
yet serve us in enabling us to become more fully human.
In the list mentioned above, Barth even includes death in
these experiences, meaning by this not death as we now
experience it in our fallen state (that is death in alienation)
but rather the cessation of earthly existence which we
would have experienced in fellowship with God had we
not fallen, but containing nonetheless its own challenges.
Through these experiences of being on the boundary we
actually experience growth to maturity and therefore
should confess them as good. But evil is that power at work
in the world about which nothing good should be said or
thought. For this irrational, absurd and destructive power
human beings should entertain nothing but scorn.

How does this concept help us in understanding physical
evil? It asserts that there is a Shadow in creation which
consists in decay, death and conflict. Properly described,
this Shadow should not be called evil. It is dark, but it is
not evil because it is created by God and provides the kind
of environment in which mankind may learn to depend
upon God. The world as we know it is substantially as
God made it. But into this world has come an alien power
which is genuinely evil. Therefore although the world of
nature is substantially as God made it, there are forces at
work which are purely destructive. This may account for
those aspects in nature which involve meaningless pain
and suffering. We cannot credit the force of evil with too
much power to affect creation, but it does have some power
to disorder and distort. From our present vantage point it
is difficult to disentangle evil from the Shadow and therefore what belongs to either will only finally be disclosed at
the end, when God's purposes are fulfilled. What we do

know is that the time is coming when the creation itself will lose its shadow side of decay and death and enter into liberty, but it will only do so in fellowship with the children of God at the consummation of all things.[38]

The conclusion of this discussion is: not all 'pain' is evil, but evil uses pain as an alibi and disguises itself behind it. Some pain is evil — the kind which is meaningless, irrational and essentially cruel, with no 'soul-making' purpose in view. A great deal of pain which is experienced in and inflicted by the human race can be seen to fit into this evil category. This approach to the problem of physical evil enables us to affirm the soul-making value of mankind facing a creation which is in some respects threatening and dark and yet which is essentially good. It also enables us to recognise evil for what it is and to reject it. It will be noticed that this approach is consistent with the idea of a pre-human angelic fall and with a serious view of the fall of mankind into moral evil. This has introduced its own kind of distortion and disruption into the creation as mankind has achieved greater and greater capacity to exploit and spoil the environment. It may also be seen that this approach escapes from the need to explain away the presence of decay and death in the creation before the fall of Adam. It therefore avoids the contortionism of some varieties of scientific creationism and fits more easily into the description of the world and its development which is given in modern scientific research.

Have we then given a sufficient answer to the problem of evil? Despite all the discussion of this chapter the answer must be No. There is no straightforward answer to the problem of evil. It may be that we can give an intellectual response which shows how Christians may consistently and honestly believe in a God who is both almighty and all-loving. The free-will defence enables this to happen. But beyond the arguments there is the fact of meaningless and mindless evil which needs a different kind of answer from that which philosophy can give. The kind of suffering faced by Eli Wiesel and millions of others cannot be understood easily. This is the point where words reach their useful limit. Of course, the very irrationality and absurdity of evil means that we will always struggle to comprehend it rationally. The difficulty in explaining it has got more than a little to do with its essential nature as that which defies reason and explanation and flies in the face of sense and meaning.

However, beyond all of this we need to point to the fact that the God who is revealed in Jesus and who has created us is not removed from human suffering. The idea that God is an impassible Being who is untouched by our pain is a false one. The God who is revealed in the cross of Jesus is one who has embraced our human suffering. He knows what it is to be rejected and to suffer. In some way which defies explanation we must assert that God is with us even when, perhaps most especially when, we experience pain and sorrow and do not understand why. Eli Wiesel goes on in his book to record a most horrific incident in the death camp where he experienced hell on earth. He describes how two men and a child were hanged before the camp. The two men were defiant in death, but the child remained silent. As they were made to watch the scene one of the camp inmates cried out 'Where is God? Where is He now?' The men were to die quickly but because he was so light the child did not die so easily.

For more than half an hour he stayed there, struggling between life and death, dying in slow agony under our eyes. And we had to look him full in the face. He was still alive when I passed in front of him. His tongue was still red, his eyes were not yet glazed. Behind me, I heard the same man asking: 'Where is God now?' And I heard a voice within me answer him: 'Where is He? Here He is — He is hanging here on this gallows. . . '[39]

It belongs to the mystery of the book as to whether Wiesel means that God also has died, or whether in some profoundly mysterious way he means that the God who knows about suffering is with those who suffer. God is the God of the cross, the crucified God who has suffered with and for men in order that he may be the Father of those who suffer. What Christians can offer in the face of suffering is not a philosophical answer to mankind's vulnerability to suffering caused through the power of evil. Rather it is faith in the God of the cross and resurrection who alone has conquered evil and is able to make it against its own nature serve the good of his creatures.

REFERENCES

1. Eli Wiesel *Night* (London, 1981) p45.
2. ibid p79.
3. *Hume's Dialogues Concerning Natural Religion* Norman Kemp Smith (Ed) (London and Edinburgh, 1947) pp193–202.
4. There appears to be some confusion about the use of the term 'metaphysical evil' with some commentators using it to refer to 'the basic fact of finitude and limitation within the created universe'. See John Hick *Evil and the God of Love* (London, 1966) p19.
5. Quoted by N. L. Geisler *The Roots of Evil* (Grand Rapids, 1978) p17.
6. *New Dictionary of Theology* (Leicester, 1988) p381.
7. Heb 12:11.
8. Rom 8:28.
9. John A. Sanford *Evil, the Shadow Side of Reality* (New York, 1981).
10. ibid p10.
11. ibid p9.
12. ibid p55.
13. ibid p40.
14. C. G. Jung *Letters (2)* (Priceton, 1975) p61 cited by Sanford *op cit* p139.

15. Sanford *op cit* p139.
16. Alvin Plantinga *God, Freedom and Evil* (Grand Rapids, 1974) p54. This book is a cogent restatement of the free will defence.
17. John Hick *Philosophy of Religion* (New Jersey, 1973) p43.
18. Col 1:20; Rev 21:1–4.
19. Rom 8:28.
20. Hick *Evil and the God of Love* p92.
21. Gen 1:26.
22. Ps 8:6–8.
23. Gen 3:17–19, 23–24.
24. *Institutes* II:1:5.
25. Gen 1:31.
26. N. M. de S. Cameron *Evolution and the Authority of the Bible* (Exeter, 1983) pp70–71.
27. Gen 5:24.
28. Bruce Milne *Know The Truth* (Leicester, 1982) p83.
29. Alvin Plantinga *God, Freedom and Evil* p58.
30. Lk 13:16.
31. C. S. Lewis *The Problem of Pain* (London, 1941) p123.
32. ibid p124.
33. Barth CD III/3 pp295–302.
34. ibid p296. See also CD III/1 p377.
35. CD III/1 p320.
36. ibid pp371–377.
37. CD III/3 p299.
38. Rom 8:18–21.
39. Wiesel *op cit* pp76–77.

CHAPTER SIX

Inside Information?

So far we have been attempting to gain a perspective on the power of darkness which will help us to see it for what it is, neither exaggerating and exalting its power nor minimising and disregarding it. We have attempted to unmask the nature of evil and the form it takes in our world. On the basis of what we have so far discussed, it is our intention to examine the activity of evil and to suggest ways in which through the crucified, risen and exalted Christ its work may be undone.

It is at this point of our enquiry that we are particularly reflecting upon the progress of charismatic renewal since it is largely, but not exclusively, in charismatic circles that the awareness of the demonic has come into prominence. This ought not to be surprising for at least two reasons. Firstly, the charismatic movement is essentially concerned with the renewal of the Spirit's power in the church. It bears testimony to a quickening of God's power in the experience of Christians and in mission to the world. If this claim be true it should not be surprising that the renewal of spiritual power should lead to conflict with opposing powers in the world. Secondly, the renewing work of the Spirit brings with it a renewal of his gifts, such as those described in 1 Corinthians 12:7–11. One of the gifts listed here is that of 'the ability to distinguish between spirits' (v10). Arnold Bittlinger understands this as the 'ability to distinguish between divine, human and demonic powers' and sees this gift manifested in the encounter of Peter with Simon Magus (Acts 8:20f) and his exposure of Ananias and Sapphira (Acts 5:3). Paul exhibits the gift in his recognition that Bar-Jesus is a son of the devil (Acts 13:10) and in perceiving that the slave girl in Philippi was controlled by a spirit of divination (Acts 16:17f).[1] If this gift is being rekindled in the church it should be no surprise if it occasionally turns up results.

It is largely through charismatic renewal therefore that the awareness of demonic powers has been stimulated in the church and it was early in the movement that the theme began to come into prominence.[2] For many Christians the ground had already been prepared for this emphasis in the popular writings of C. S. Lewis who expressed the theme in both his fictional and apologetic writings.[3]

In more recent years the theme of spiritual warfare has broadened out. The concern for many charismatic groups has become corporate spiritual warfare operating with the belief that there are powers of darkness which can control and dominate society. These powers are to be engaged and confronted with words of authority which throw back their influence and reclaim the territory for God. This process is sometimes carried out by means of 'Make Way' marches which are designed to proclaim the Lordship of Christ in localities thereby reinforcing the dethroning of the dark powers which afflict society. This new philosophy of spiritual warfare will be the subject of a later chapter. It serves to indicate that the conception of spiritual warfare that is to be found in charismatic circles is in a process of development.

In this chapter the intention is to examine the claims

that are made about the nature of demonic interference in the lives of individuals, the area usually called 'demon possession' or 'oppression' the solution to which is known as 'deliverance'. More recently the tendency has been to refer to 'demonisation' as this is more biblically accurate[4] and more suitable pastorally in that it indicates the imprecise nature of much demonic interference. The method we follow will be to examine four differing accounts of the phenomenon of demonisation and its remedy in deliverance ministry before going on to attempt to understand what is being claimed.

1. Four accounts of demonisation

(a) *The Blumhardt experience.* We begin with an experience which is not well known and yet which has exercised a profound influence in the German speaking world. This is the remarkable story of a Lutheran pastor called Johann Christoph Blumhardt (1805–80) who ministered at a village called Moettlingen from 1838–52. Blumhardt belonged to the Pietist wing of the Lutheran church which emphasized the need for experience of God, but he was not typical of this tradition preserving a strong emphasis upon the objective work of Christ and a universal hope for the world. While in Moettlingen he unexpectedly experienced a very dramatic encounter with demonic forces afflicting a parishioner called Gottliebin Dittus. He was later to describe his two-year struggle to rescue this woman in a report to his local synod.[5] In measured and sober terms he describes how Gottliebin, a devout and otherwise unremarkable woman of twenty-eight, suffered from various physical ailments and began from 1840 to experience strange phenomena in her apartment along with disturbing physical interference. The phenomena included the appearance of figures, noises in the house and the materialization of objects. When prayed for she would experience convulsions. Blumhardt became convinced that these were demonic in origin and after declaring 'we have seen long enough what the devil is doing, now we also want to see what Jesus can do' things took a major turn for the better.[6] The pattern of convulsion and prayer leading to deliverance continued, accompanied by the most bizarre and horrific phenomena, for some time. Demons spoke out of her claiming to be the spirits of deceased persons and angels of Satan.[7] Gottliebin's sister, Katharina, and her brother also began to show symptoms of similar demonization until the final moment of deliverance came on 28 December 1843. The battle centred at this point around Katharina. Blumhardt writes:

> Finally the most moving moment came which no-one can possibly imagine who was not an eye and ear witness. At two o'clock in the morning the supposed angel of Satan roared, while the girl bent back her head and upper part of her body over the backrest of the chair, with a voice of which one would hardly have believed a human throat capable, 'Jesus is Victor! Jesus is Victor!' — words that sounded so far and were understood at such a distance that they made an unforgettable impression on many people. Now the power and strength of the demon seemed to be broken more with every moment. It became ever more quiet and calmer, could only make a few motions and finally disappeared unnoticed like the life-light of a dying person goes out.[8]

The outcome of the conflict was that the family were restored to a peaceful and healthful state. Gottliebin recovered from all her former illnesses to develop as a deeply spiritual person with a loving and kindly ministry as a schoolteacher.[9] The impact of the incident was such as to spark off a wave of spiritual renewal. Blumhardt became a popular preacher and between 1852–80 the leader of a renewal centre at Bad Boll which played the same kind of role in Germany that Keswick played in England. The characteristic theme of the renewal movement was the phrase Jesus is Victor!, a phrase later picked up and extensively used by the theologian Karl Barth, prompting the comment 'the voice of the devil is an unexpected source for modern theology'![10]

The most remarkable aspect of this whole story is to trace the effect of Blumhardt and his son Christoph Friedrich on twentieth century theology. Barth was decisively influenced by them at the time of his own theological revolution during the First World War.[11] Emil Brunner, Oscar Cullmann, Dietrich Bonhoeffer are all among theologians who acknowledge a debt to the Blumhardt inheritance.[12] All of this would indicate that the 'murky performances at Moettlingen'[13] should not be too easily dismissed as the superstitious and naive interpretations of an unsophisticated country parson. Blumhardt was sober, intelligent, educated, accurate and highly respected. Nothing in the circumstances of his life or in the spirit of the age would have predisposed him to find demons in his parishioner. For him it was unexpected and unlooked for.

> Although I trembled through every paragraph, thinking whether it might not be hasty and careless to tell everything so clearly, I felt the urge within me again and again, 'Tell it all'.[14]

(b) *War on the Saints.* In 1904 the Welsh Revival led to the conversion of large numbers and had a profound impact on the social life of the people. An estimated one hundred thousand were converted. One of the chief human instruments in the revival was Evan Roberts who himself paid such a physical price that his health was broken and he lived a life of retirement until his death in 1951.[15] Another major figure was Jessie Penn-Lewis who wrote a book in collaboration with Roberts entitled *War on the Saints* detailing experiences which were encountered in the wake of the revival.[16] The book is a highly detailed description of the deceptive workings of the powers of darkness. The thesis with which the book operates is that demons are at work in abundance, deceiving and possessing individuals, including Christians.[17] Indeed a particular danger point is when a Christian is baptised in the Holy Spirit since it is at this point of abandonment to the invisible and supernatural that he or she becomes vulnerable to deception.[18] Evil spirits either prior to or after this time, gain access to the body or mind and hide deeply in the structure of the person becoming to all intents and purposes part of them. It is the lack of discernment and ignorance of Christians that renders them so vulnerable.[19]

War on the Saints is a disturbing book. This is partly because it points in the direction of genuine dangers. It came out of the spiritual turbulence that occurred in the aftermath of the revival. As in previous times of revival it became clear that not all the phenomena which accompanied it were without their problems. There were counterfeits. There was mixture of good and bad in the experience of those who had been visited. Many of the phenomena which were considered by some to be signs of the presence of God were seen in time to be spurious. These observations need to be reflected upon. But the book is disturbing for another reason, namely the picture it draws of the almost complete vulnerability of ordinary Christians to demonic attack. If the danger of deception is so great, it is only the mature and discerning (and perhaps not even they?) who are in a position to withstand. We are left with a rather hopeless picture of a church in which the ordinary person is acted upon by both good and evil powers in a highly exposed way. After all, if to be baptized in the Holy Spirit renders a person vulnerable to invisible and supernatural invasion by the enemy, what hope is there for any of us? Where is the sense of security in openness to the Father? Where is the comfort given by Jesus to the effect that 'nothing will harm you'?[20]

It is here that we begin to see the need for the ground work that we have attempted in the earlier parts of this book. Whatever valuable insights may be contained in Mrs Penn-Lewis's book (and there are many), there is such a concentration on the demonic and such a ready acceptance of the power of the enemy that this way of thinking actually serves to increase the power of the enemy who is otherwise so energetically resisted. The world becomes the province of demons and a 'demon consciousness' is encouraged which gives them an attention and a respect that they thrive and trade upon. In preference to this we need to assume the position of scorn and of radical disbelief in relation to the demonic.

(c) *Pigs in the Parlour.* In 1973 Frank and Ida Hammond published a book entitled *Pigs in the Parlour* describing their experience of deliverance ministry and seeking to give some practical guidance in this area.[21] At that time Frank Hammond had enjoyed twenty-five years as a Baptist pastor, held two degrees and had only recently entered onto the deliverance realm. The title of the book draws a parallel between the unclean swine of the Old Testament and evil spirits in the New. The need for deliverance is, in their opinion, very widespread. Indeed, Frank writes: 'Does everyone need deliverance? Personally, I have not found any exceptions.'[22] Satan's kingdom is an organised one. It involves a 'prince spirit' set over each local church and which accounts for the specific types of problem faced by it on a recurring basis. Examples of these include 'doctrinal demons', or demons of false doctrine (1 Tim 4:1). Likewise, nations and communities have 'ruling demon potentates' along the lines of the 'prince of Persia' against which Michael the archangel fought (Dan 10:13). Demons operate in rough groupings and it is common to find clusters of spirits of a similar type infesting an individual.[23] Certain combinations of spirits can be found working together for instance to produce schizophrenia.[24] When this is understood by the deliverance minister it becomes possible to root out the spirits which afflict in this way. Deliverance is generally assisted by being able to identify a spirit by name and command it specifically to leave. This may be done by one who ministers, by oneself or even by proxy for another.[25] According to the book, when deliverance is engaged in, the exit of the demon takes place through the mouth or nose and may be indicated by the expulsion of breath or by coughing.[26] Even children need deliverance, but this normally is more easily achieved.[27]

What the Hammonds present us with is a picture of a world in which demons are highly active and where many ailments both physical and mental actually have their root in demonisation. The extensive picture of the demonic kingdom which is described is one which has been discovered by the actual experience of ministering deliverance. This raises the question of how much credibility can be given to the experience of individuals when there is little or no biblical warrant for the kinds of detailed descriptions they go in for. Generally, the book demonstrates a very literal approach to Scripture as can be perceived in the odd remarks which are made about the sinister nature of owls and frogs. Concern is expressed that these creatures, described in Deuteronomy 14:7–19 as unclean and regarded as types of evil spirits, are being made into art objects and decorations. The fact that such creatures are animals of the night also counts against them![28] Remarks such as this indicate that there is a form of biblical naivety at work here and does not evidence a large amount of theological acumen.

(d) *Demons Defeated.* A further book that has enjoyed popularity recently was written by New Zealand lawyer and Anglican lay person, Bill Subritzky. Like the Hammonds he describes his own discovery of the deliverance ministry, in his case through his son's deliverance.[29] Approaching Scripture in an unsophisticated and highly subjective way, he describes how 'Satan places unseen princes and powers of the air over every nation and city with descending orders of authority all the way down to demons which walk on the ground and seek a home'.[30] There are three primary 'strong men', or spiritual forces, which Subritzky names as the spirits of Jezebel, Antichrist, and Death and Hell. Together these are the Satanic counterparts of the Holy Trinity.[31] Under the direction of these strong men, demons are highly active in the world and can enter people in many ways, including through heredity, parental rejection, contact with demonised persons, curses and rock music.[32] When ministering deliverance it is helpful, according to Subritzky, to recognise that there is a 'leader of the pack' among the demons. Frequently this is one of the strong men mentioned above. Other demons, some of them with identical names will cluster around this leader.[33] In the deliverance process, the presence of angels is an occasional experience.[34] Once delivered it is essential to live a sanctified life in order to keep the deliverance which has been received.[35]

The purpose of reviewing these books has not been to give an exhaustive analysis of them but simply to indicate the way of thinking that they adopt. The last three books in particular have exercised a wide, popular influence and are referred to by many as formative of their thinking in this area. They clearly indicate particular (and perhaps idiosyncratic) points of view both in the interpretation and application of Scripture. It is possible to refer to other books on the popular level,[36] and some of a more substantial nature,[37] which cover the same ground, albeit with variations. However, these approaches raise immense questions. If what these books appear to describe is true, then a radical readjustment is necessary in our way of looking at the world and in our method of ministry within it. If on the other hand it is mistaken, we are being led into areas of superstition and delusion which will not profit in any way at all. What are we to make of it all? We shall proceed by examining some objections to this approach and attempting to make our way through the minefield. The conclusion we shall reach is that demonisation is a reality and we need to know how to deal with it — but we need to take great care that it does not get out of hand.

2. Dealing with the difficulties

(a) No return to the Dark Ages. One straightforward response to the above accounts of demonisation and deliverance is simply to reject it as a load of nonsense perpetrated by credulous and deluded individuals. A world populated by demons in the ways described is to be rejected as primitive, pre-scientific and pre-Enlightenment, and not to be entertained by thinking people in the twentieth century. What is needed today is not deliverance from evil spirits but deliverance from *belief* in them. When this whole area was discussed in the mid-1970s Professor Geoffrey Lampe and Mr Don Cupitt produced an open letter signed by sixty-five theologians which asserted:

It is, we think, mistaken to suppose that loyalty to Christ

requires the Church to recreate, in late twentieth century Europe, the outlook and practices of first century Palestine. Such an attempt invites ridicule, not to mention the harm that may be done. We urge all who hold high office in the Church to ensure that the practice of exorcism receives no official encouragement and gains no official status in the Church.[38]

According to this viewpoint, belief in spirits is not binding on Christians today simply because Jesus believed in them any more than it is mandatory for Christians to wear sandals, robes and long hair. It is based on the views that in the ancient world everybody believed in spirits and today nobody with any grasp of the modern worldview does. However, both these points of view are suspect. Firstly, not everybody in the ancient world believed in the existence of demons and therefore the fact that Jesus did is significant. Secondly, there is much evidence to indicate that the scientific worldview does not adequately explain the total experience of mankind today and that therefore belief in dark powers is still a serviceable way of making sense of some aspects of actual experience. The first and twentieth centuries are not so different as might be supposed.[39] Accepting the reality of demons still remains a coherent way of describing reality.

Furthermore, what this dogmatic approach must find an explanation for is the fact that those who speak of demons are not necessarily unintelligent and credulous people. It may be that some of the literature produced creates this impression. But such literature is only part of a wider body of research in which highly educated and intelligent people from a broad spectrum of disciplines argue forcibly for the reality of this realm.[40] What must be accepted is that people experience phenomena of such intensity and of such a type that it is possible to identify those present day experiences with those described in the New Testament. These experiences are such that the only adequate explanation appears to be that of demonisation. This impression is gained not least because of the clearly overpowering nature of what some individuals experience, because of the ability of the invading entity to speak through the voice of the individual concerned and because of a clear antipathy towards anything to do with Christ whether this be mention of his name or of his work. It is the inexplicability of these experiences by reference to other theories and supremely the fact that ministry in the name of Jesus actually sets people free, that has led large numbers of Christian ministers to revise their previously held sceptical views in this area.

(b) Going beyond scripture. A second objection is concerned with the fact that demonology is becoming an area for investigation when the Bible has little to say about it other than incidentally. This is a weighty objection. Whereas a central theme in the Bible is that Christ has come to destroy the work of the devil, the Bible does not seem to be interested in the kind of demonology that certain individuals have come to specialise in and be 'authorities' on. There is something objectionable about investigating something which the Bible considers not worth it. It is to be regarded as particularly disturbing when knowledge of the demonic 'kingdom' is not derived from Christ but from demons themselves by information they impart as to their own identity and activity. Is not this kind of inside information intrinsically wrong? And are not demons such inherently deceitful entities that an element of distortion is bound to be present in anything derived from this realm? This is a matter of such major importance that a number of cautionary assertions are essential.

(i) We need to assert that the New Testament shows no interest in demonology as such and only treats it as an incidental to the positive work of Christ in bringing the kingdom of God. This is not to say that the expulsion of demons was a peripheral part of Christ's ministry. It clearly was both important and central, but it was one element of a total work of forgiveness, healing and liberation. In the church's ministry today we should expect it to be one, but only one, element of our work.

(ii) The New Testament says very little about the internal workings of the kingdom of darkness and this should lead us to take a somewhat agnostic position in regard to any particular account of how the demonic world ticks. Where truth is revealed in Scripture we can take an unequivocal stand upon it. Where it is not we must sit loose to anything that claims to 'tell it as it is'. The books that attempt to do this should not be taken as authoritative but as attempts to describe and make sense of experience which are bound to be defective to a greater or lesser degree. This is not to say that such experience is invalid simply because the Bible does not mention it. The Bible knows nothing, for instance of the post-Freudian account of the working of the human personality. Yet it is taken for granted today that the kind of knowledge and understanding that can be gained through psychology and psychiatry are essential for wise pastoral care. We should accept that there is knowledge which may be gained in the practice of the Christian life of which the Bible does not specifically speak. Indeed there is an analogy here with the counselling disciplines. The proponents of the various schools of counselling tend to think that they each have the right approach. Yet in reality each account offers a model which is at best only an imprecise way of understanding the workings of the human soul. We should take the same attitude towards the various descriptions of deliverance. Nobody has the ultimate viewpoint. Some may have got it completely wrong.

(iii) There is a third factor which is of crucial importance. It is a mistake to conceive of the demonic realm as well organised and highly structured. Its essence is not reason but unreason, not organisation but chaos. 'The inconsistent, incoherent and chaotic nature of evil besets an enquiry into the existence of demons so that one's results will have to remain tentative.'[41] Given this we should expect that demonic activity may change from place to place, from age to age and from moment to moment. Accounts that outline the shape of the demonic organisation are to be treated with extreme scepticism.

(iv) This last point must be followed up by a further one of the same kind. We need to *beware of the danger of finding what we expect to find in this realm*. This is the reverse side of the danger of not finding what we don't believe we can or should find. All counsellors will be aware of the danger of imposing their own expectations and models upon their counsellees. It is a matter of human fact that given the kind of reciprocal relationship which makes counselling possible, counsellees will knowingly or unknowingly come up with the goods that their counsellors appear to be looking for. If we have too clear a notion of what we are looking for in the demonic realm it ought to come as no surprise if we keep on finding it. There are intricate and subtle interpersonal factors at work here.

These cautionary words are designed to help us hold fast to Scripture and to sit loose to everything else. At the same time it is possible to exaggerate the silence of Scripture in this field. Encounter with the demonic often leads to renewed reflection on the details of the biblical accounts. It can be quite easily deduced that demonisation might involve large numbers of demonic entities (eg 'Legion'), that they produce symptoms of madness and distress as well as physical illness, that there are different kinds of demons, and that some are particularly difficult to get rid of (Mt 17:21), that they are capable of speaking through individuals, and that they can produce extraordinary violence in those they infest (Acts 19:14–16). Nevertheless, all of these details are incidental and the balance of the New Testament is worthy of imitation in that whereas it accepts the reality of the demonic it never shows more than a passing interest in it. In the light of this it is to be seriously questioned whether it is spiritually profitable to publish books, produce tapes or run courses in this area other than those which are of the most restrained kind. The effect of these is all too often to create an unhealthy 'demon mentality' in over-receptive minds.

(c) The paranoid worldview. This brings us to a third objection. If the world really is so highly infested with demons as some suggest, what are the implications of this for the way we look at the world? Is not this tendency to attribute so much activity to the demons imminently in danger of pandering to the paranoia, the mental delusion of persecution and conspiracy, which is characteristic of the neurotic personality and which lurks not far beneath the surface of most of us? The force of this criticism is considerable, particularly in the light of pastoral experience which indicates that there are those, often of a neurotic disposition or with a liking for conspiracy theories, who see demons everywhere. It is to counteract this tendency that this book is being written. The fact that it is being attempted is a sign that there is, for some, a problem at this point. And if the vocabulary and thought forms Christians use stimulate this morbid neurosis we need to pay attention to both.

For the moment our concern is firmly with demonisation

in its individual expression and with counteracting 'demonomania', the over-inclination to explain things in terms of the demonic. One way we can do this is to ask, how frequent is demonisation? According to Frank Hammond, as we have seen, everybody in his experience is demonised to some degree. Subritzky and Penn-Lewis would see it as very widespread. The worrying aspect of this tendency is the way in which there seems to be little concept of wider factors that may be involved in the spiritual, mental and social health of those concerned. Demons have become the grid through which personal problems are viewed.

Others who accept the reality of demonisation nevertheless see it as a rare occurrence. In the report of the Christian Exorcism Study Group, which can scarcely be described as unspiritually sceptical, possession by an evil spirit is held to take place only when the individual puts him or herself in a vulnerable position and deliberately invites invasion. It may also occur through indirect contact with blatant forms of the occult.[42] A previous report on exorcism edited by Dom Robert Petitpierre also sees possession as very rare, although real.[43] A psychiatrist with wide experience in this field put the number of his patients needing exorcism at around four per cent.[44] Another psychiatrist is quite sceptical, finding the many cases cited by Kurt Koch 'very unconvincing'.[45]

Part of this wide discrepancy among those who are disposed to accept the possibility of demonic interference may of course be explained by a different way of understanding what is meant by 'possession'. For some, it is the extreme point of a spectrum of demonic onslaught ranging from temptation through obsession and oppression to possession.[46] It is therefore rare. Others reject 'possession' language and speak rather in terms of demonisation to refer to forms of demonic penetration to a greater or lesser degree. The equation requires however that wherever there is some penetration of sin (that is everywhere) there will be some demonic interference.[47] A Christian therefore, could never be 'demon possessed' since this would imply ownership by demons, but he or she could be trespassed upon unlawfully by demons.[48] This takes us into areas we have yet to discuss. The point is that even beyond the different use of terms and the differing concepts there is disagreement concerning the degree to which demons are active in the world. Some are inclined to see demons as a sinister element in a total picture of human fallenness. Others see them as the primary agents of all forms of human sin and affliction. The point here is that the former of these attitudes is by far the healthier to entertain. It is healthier because it does not lead to demonomania in a way that the second attitude will surely do but takes more seriously the role of human responsibility. It also avoids giving to demons a glory which is not theirs. The notion that demons are as active as some would wish to suppose is a simplistic approach which does not take seriously enough the other dimensions of human nature and sin. This brings us to a further objection in this area.

(d) Cannot 'demonisation' be adequately explained in other ways? Here is a major question. Granted that those who deal with demons are experiencing *something* which looks like demonisation, have they got the right interpretation of the phenomenon they are observing? And have they got the right interpretation in every case? Could it not be explained quite adequately by reference to psychological factors? Furthermore, if this is the case it becomes dangerous and pastorally irresponsible in the extreme to suggest to people (who may be very open to suggestion) that they have a demon problem. A Christian psychiatrist, Dr Monty Barker, draws attention to a group of twenty disturbed people for whom he was clinically responsible, the average age of whom was twenty-two, with high intelligence and mainly Christian background. 'A high proportion had been in contact with charismatic groups. A number had had the idea suggested to them that they were possessed. Some had received exorcism, one on three occasions.'[49] The conclusion he came to was that none of them was demonised but that those who felt themselves to be so were externalising their own conflicts and distresses as demons. In this way 'the search for solutions can be given up and responsibility handed over to the demons and to the exorcist.'[50]

It is plain that we are in a complex realm where even angels should fear to tread. This should warn us against simplistic explanations of complex human reactions. In attempting to gain perspective here I intend to venture some tentative reflections drawn from some experience in this realm. When ministering in this area we need to keep the following factors firmly in our minds.

(i) *Human beings are psychologically more complex than we imagine*. Put briefly, an individual can manifest all the symptoms of demonization when in reality their difficulties are psychological in origin. To treat such persons as if they were demonized is both to confirm their false perception of the situation and to collude with them in it. It is to commit a grave pastoral error which is invasive of their personality. The strange forms of behaviour which might lead the unskilled person to assume demonic activity may therefore indicate nothing more than a disordered inner life with complex psychological origins. The power of the unconscious in humans is immense and out of it can come the most surprising things including the kinds of reactions which may on the face of it look demonic. In reality these reactions may be repressed emotions, buried hurts, unacknowledged frustrations or complex elements of their personality which have been denied, split off and made into autonomous elements of the person's inner being.[51] The point I am making is that the same symptoms may be produced by different causes. To complicate the issue further is the fact that some people enjoy the kind of intense attention which is given to those afflicted by demons and therefore will produce the symptoms for as long as it gains them attention. There are also those who for the worst of reasons seek to absorb the time and energy of Christian people to divert them from other tasks.

(ii) *Human beings are socially more complex than we imagine.* Here I am opening up two possibilities. The first is that of suggestibility. In the kind of dependent and trusting relationships that develop between individuals in need and their counsellors there can enter in a form of illusion. The counsellee responds to the suggestions of the counsellor and produces the kind of responses which are felt to be expected. Thereby he or she confirms the expectations of the counsellor and the cycle goes on. It is not uncommon in the sphere of deliverance to observe a form of bonding between counsellor and counsellee whereby there is a merging of conceptual horizons, a sense of solidarity against the rest of the world and a consequent loss of the kind of critical objectivity which would enable there to be a retreat from a misdiagnosis towards a more adequate diagnosis. The counsellee wishes to avoid questioning the counsellor and the counsellor cannot face the possible disappointment of the counsellee. Neither dare appear 'unspiritual' by suggesting a natural rather than supernatural cause for the presenting symptoms. When this dynamic is compounded by the involvement of others who are convinced about the demonic cause, a situation has been produced which it is difficult to extricate oneself from.

The second possibility is that an individual may become the victim of a group mentality which is 'demon-minded' and imprisons certain individuals within this thought form. If the dominant ethos of a group, church or otherwise, is inclined to find demons at work and perceives a group member's problem to be along these lines, the group pressure may prove too difficult to resist. The victim is faced with the choice of forsaking the group, with all the emotional difficulties that would entail, or of obediently playing along and producing the appropriate forms of behaviour. It must be stressed that this process operates primarily on the subconscious level and therefore an individual may be totally unconscious of what is actually happening. When this does happen it is not surprising if the individual is carried along by the group for some time before finding the burden intolerable and opting out.

(iii)*Human beings are psychically more complex than we imagine.* No doubt some readers will imagine that in this section I go too far but I am attempting to be true to pastoral experiences. It is a feature of revivals and powerful spiritual visitations that in the wake of a genuine movement of the Spirit there are phenomena which are spurious. Jonathan Edwards wrote a major treatise on this subject after the eighteenth century revival in New England when some of the post-revival phenomena threatened to bring the revival into question as a genuine work of God.[52] Precisely the same problem was experienced after the Welsh Revival of 1904 which was strongly marked by spiritual ferment and physical manifestations of the presence of God's Spirit. It is no part of my intention to cast doubt on the validity of such happenings but rather to draw attention to the aftermath in which phenomena that are not the result of the action of the Spirit can continue, as it were, under their own steam. Martyn Lloyd-Jones, a keen student and advocate of revival, described this possibility as 'the danger of passing from the spiritual to the psychological and possibly even the psychic'.[53]

In all spiritual affairs we need to be aware of the possibility that phenomena which exceed the conscious capacity and ability of individuals may actually have their origin not in the Spirit of God nor necessarily in evil spirits but simply in forms of psychic energy which are deeper even than the subconscious mind. In saying this I am aware that scientific definitions of the human psyche do not have much place for what I am calling the 'psychic'. It appears to me however that it is necessary to speak of such a dimension in order to explain the facts of my own pastoral experience and that of others. It is significant that the report of the Christian Exorcism Study Group takes this energy source with considerable seriousness and finds it possible to explain much paranormal activity (but not all) without reference to the demonic. It has its origin in the psychic reservoirs that some people develop the ability to tap. This human origin does not make development of this area acceptable since the Christian revelation calls for dependence on God and devotion to him instead of it. Manipulations of the psychic were forbidden in Scripture 'because they involved a divided loyalty to the Lord, and therefore hampered people from developing along the lines God willed'.[54] The realm of the psychic may be regarded as neither holy nor demonic in itself but when orientated towards God it becomes integrated with the total life in communion with God. When orientated towards the devil it becomes the realm of unwholesome demonic activity. When not surrendered to God and even if not consciously surrendered to darkness, it remains an area which is invadable by darkness to greater or lesser degrees depending upon the residual character and will of the individual. For this reason to develop this area independently of God is fraught with dangers. Even for the Christian the realm of the psychic should not be developed independently or self-consciously but should simply take its place in the yielding of the total person to God's Spirit thus finding its true integration in the total person and especially in unity with the mind and in the Spirit of God.

The point of this extended (but important) discussion is to indicate that the inner life of people is also complex. For this reason we are told to test the spirits. Not all unusual and apparently 'spiritual' phenomena are properly of God. They may be psychic. Conversely, not all apparently sinister 'spiritual' occurrences are demonic. They also may be psychic in nature. From this several conclusions are to be drawn. Firstly, there is the possibility that phenomena, which are taken in deliverance ministry to be demons, are in fact to be understood as elements of 'psychic turbulence' which will react to exorcism but for which exorcism is inappropriate. What I have in mind here is that in a deliverance situation, words of authority spoken by authoritative figures who are well respected and which are addressed to the subconscious may very well produce an effect and cause a reaction. It may be that such words may confront an area of sinfulness, or hurt or long repressed and forgotten memories and thus produce a result which resembles a demonic deliverance. Yet to see it as such is to misunderstand it.

Secondly, it may be that given such a situation of deliverance ministry an individual is without knowing it pushed into areas of imagination where they fantasise events and incidents which have a certain coherence. The imagination is of course fed by what has been seen, heard and read over many years as well as by that of which the imagination functioning on the boundary is naturally capable. While receiving ministry, a counsellee may well therefore supply the counsellor with plausible but unreal stories of demonic intrigue which at the time are believed to be true.

Thirdly, the situation is to be imagined where an individual is actually demonised and receives liberating ministry. But having under demonic influence reacted in certain ways to the ministry received (shaking, coughing, groaning and the like) continues to respond to further prayer and ministry in this way not because they are still demonised but because they have entered subconsciously or psychically into an autonomic response to the personalities involved and the words used in the counselling situation. Where this is the case exorcism is no longer appropriate and needs to be replaced by a form of therapy which will help the individual to return to an ordered and peaceful existence.

(iv)*Human beings are spiritually more complex than we imagine.* We have already touched upon this fact in the previous section. The intention here is to underline it by arguing that, in addition to the devil, Christians war against the flesh. The 'flesh' can account for many of the phenomena which are described by the incautious as demonic. To illustrate this it is helpful to refer to the ambiguity of the word 'spirit'. This word can be used to describe an evil spirit or it can indicate an attitude or an underlying disposition. We may therefore speak of a 'spirit of pride' or a 'spirit of gluttony' without at all intending to describe a demonic entity but rather a sinful power which has gained a foothold in an individual or a group. If this is the case then deliverance or liberation from a concrete form of sin is needed and by virtue of its having become a binding power there may be a superficial resemblance to a demon. Deliverance therefore should be seen as a spectrum which extends at one end from the foothold that sin may have gained through ingrained habit or enslavement through to actual and specific demonisation. In a deliverance context such binding sin might react to the name of Christ and might be mistaken for an evil spirit. My suspicion is that the majority of what is taken to be demonic in the books by Hammond and Subritzky is of this nature. Deliverance from binding sin is necessary but this should not be administered under the form or under the name of exorcism.

The object of this section has been to show that the area of deliverance is one of great complexity. This does not mean it is an invalid area. It may be that deliverance ministry is inappropriate and that many cases fit into the kind of categories outlined above. It may be however that the symptoms which cause people to seek help actually do have as their cause some demonic affliction and that only this form of ministry will set them free. It may also be that few cases are clear cut and straightforward and that people may be psychologically, socially, psychically and spiritually in need and at the same time be demonically afflicted. Cardinal Suenens has written:

> The fact that a phenomenon can be explained according to our scientific categories does not allow us to rule out the possibility of an interpretation belonging to another order or level of reality. We have to remind the scientist — if he is a Christian — that there are realities and dimensions which cannot be experimentally verified and that, furthermore, scientific objectivity does not allow us to dismiss other possible explanations in our interpretation of phenomena.[55]

What we are justified in saying most clearly is that this complex area is not a place for the credulous and pastorally irresponsible. We should heed the warning of Kurt Koch that:

Convinced occultists, spiritists and sadly, often simple
and solid Christians also sometimes accept without question a belief in spirits and demons where this is
completely unnecessary. Over and against this excessive
belief in transcendent powers, we must seek the objective
facts with sobriety and realism.[56]

(e) How can Christians have demons? A fifth issue
which needs to be raised is one which divides Christian
from Christian. Deliverance ministry is practised by Christians, and this is not surprising. It is also practised on
Christians, and this is. How can Christians who are indwelt
by the Holy Spirit be demonised? Furthermore, is there
not a clash of authority at this point between those who
base their case on the Bible, which does not appear to
allow the possibility of demonised Christians, and those
who appeal to the actual experience of encountering Christians who are demonised? If we appeal to experience are
we not left with subjective opinions?

It is plain that the Bible is the court of appeal for Christian believers. But what it says on specific pastoral issues
is not always self-evident. Moreover, while experience is
not the final authority for faith, experience does have to be
made sense of. It raises questions and sheds light on the
meaning of the biblical text. It is not enough to assert
about any given experience that it contradicts the Bible. It
may just contradict what we think the Bible says. Therefore
we need to enter into the dialogue between experience and
the biblical text.

Concerning the relationship between Christians and evil
spirits, we are able to assert the following:

(i) Everybody agrees that Christians can be tempted by
the devil.

(ii) Everybody agrees that Christians are prone to sin

and have to struggle against the flesh, that is, the downward drag of those parts of our lives which remain unrenewed.

(iii) Everybody agrees that Christians cannot be 'possessed' by evil spirits since they belong to Christ.

(iv) Some hold this to mean that no evil spirits can exist within a Christian since the Christian is the temple of the Holy Spirit and evil spirits could not peacefully co-exist with the Holy Spirit.

(v) Others hold it to mean that while the spirit of the Christian, his or her innermost being, is indwelt by the Spirit, the outer regions of the person, that is the body and the outer areas of personality, can be infested. Yet a Christian cannot be possessed in an absolute sense.

(vi) Those who hold this view would not consider that such spirits could enter at will but would either be residual, that is, left over from the person's pre-Christian existence never having been expelled, or judgemental, that is, having entered as a consequence of specific disobedience. When out of fellowship with God, the individual may have made themselves vulnerable in some way.

(vii) Those who consider Christians 'demon proof' might consider it possible that under extreme circumstances they might be externally oppressed by spirits, but not internally possessed.

(viii) What we consider the Bible to teach on this matter depends partly on which verses we select. So Lk 13:16 refers to a 'daughter of Abraham' (which implies a devotion to God) who had been 'kept bound' by Satan. In Mk 8:33 Jesus rebuked Peter with the words 'Out of my sight, Satan.' These might be held to imply a degree of access possible for the devil into the life of a believer on the basis of lack of sanctification. On the other hand this is not a necessary interpretation. From a different perspective, the words of Paul in 2 Corinthians 6:14–17: 'What fellowship can light have with darkness? What harmony is there between Christ and Belial?' points to the *logical* impossibility of such fellowship, not its actual impossibility in the form of inconsistent Christian living. As it happened, the impossible possibility of Christians being wrongfully associated and involved is precisely what was happening.

(ix) The difficulties occur over this issue because of the spatial model of being indwelt by the Holy Spirit (1 Cor 3:16–17).[57] Yet this is not the only model of the Christian's experience given in the New Testament. A further model is that of the Christian as a battle zone where the Spirit of God and the sinful nature confront each other in hostility (Rom 8:5–8). This holds open the possibility that the Spirit of God may on occasion not co-exist with but confront an evil spirit across a frontier drawn across a human life.

(x) Considered in this way it does become possible to conceive of demonic strongholds in the life of an individual. If conversion is the process whereby God invades the individual life it remains true that this process is not immediately completed, otherwise we would have difficulty in accounting for the fact that Christians still do sin. The reason demonic strongholds might continue to exist after regeneration is that we have reduced and devalued the conversion process. If an inadequate gospel is preached which does not bring about heartfelt repentance and does not stress the putting off of the old life, it is not surprising that darkness is not always rooted out as it should be.

(xi) In this context, it is worth noting that ancient and some modern baptismal practices make place for clear and deliberate renunciation of the devil and all his works as part of the baptismal experience. Perhaps we need to return to this and to see the power of baptism in a new light.

3. Conclusion

There is now available a body of literature which gives
sound advice on how deliverance ministry, when it proves
to be necessary, may be carried through in a way which is
pastorally wise and sensitive. There is no need to repeat it
here.[58] However in the light of the cautionary words that
have been written in this chapter it might prove helpful to
highlight some points to supplement the literature that
already exists.

(1) It is wise to be highly reluctant to conclude that
a person is demonised. Therefore every previous avenue
normally needs to be explored before coming to this
conclusion.

(2) Deliverance ministry should never be undertaken
under pressure either from the individual concerned or
from a group. It should only be attempted if there is a
clear sense of direction and conviction from God.

(3) Wherever possible it is wise to have medical and
psychiatric support in ministering to an individual. Some
church disciplines require that permission be gained from
a higher church authority before anything is done.

(4) Where it is possible to consult a more experienced
minister this should be done. Some church structures
appoint consultants for this task.

(5) Deliverance should never be attempted alone. There
should be at least two mature and experienced Christians
present and it is preferable that one should come from
another church to provide objectivity. Obvious care needs
to be taken when ministering to members of the opposite
sex.

(6) Sessions of deliverance should not be protracted but
should be for a set time and in a suitable context. It is

important that those who minister should not find themselves being exhausted nor their home life disrupted.

(7) Intense situations of mutual dependence should be avoided and a sense of critical distance maintained about the deliverance process.

(8) Every person should be treated with gentleness and respect at all times. There should be an avoidance of aggressive words, gestures or expressions and a reliance upon the authority of Christ.

(9) Demons should not be talked to, argued with or given any attention other than that of rejecting, refusing and scorning them.

(10) The use of holy water, crosses, sacred objects, communion wine, anointing oil or the Lord's Prayer in this context should be discouraged. It is the name of Christ alone which has power and the use of physical means in a quasi-magical way heads in the wrong direction. It is not the minister who drives out demons but Christ. The name of Christ brings about the confrontation which will set people free.

(11) Deliverance should not be used for its sensation value in Christian testimony but should be discussed only when it is necessary and in a discreet, sober and undramatic way. It should not be glorified in (Lk 10:20), but seen as a necessary and routine task. It should be subject to the same ethics of confidentiality as any other form of counselling. It should take place within an accountable structure. Conversations which would elicit details for the wrong reasons should be refused.

(12) As in the ministry of Jesus the demonic factor and its remedy should not be given any more than incidental attention. 'Demonophilia' (seeing demons all over the place) is offensive to God and bad for the soul.

(13) Those who receive deliverance should be treated as individuals who bear responsibility for their own lives. It

must be recognised that their freedom is consequent upon their will to repent and be free. Deliverance is not a substitute for sturdy and responsible discipleship.

The object of all the remarks made in this chapter has been to encourage good attitudes and good practice. It is vital for the good of the renewing work taking place in the church that we get it right.

REFERENCES

1. Arnold Bittlinger *Gifts and Graces* (London, 1967) pp45–6.
2. See eg Michael Harper *Spiritual Warfare* (London, 1970).
3. See *The Screwtape Letters* (London, 1942); *Screwtape Proposes A Toast* (London, 1965); *Mere Christianity* (London, 1952).
4. The words 'demon possessed', although present in English versions are used to translate the word 'demonized' which is found in various forms some thirteen times in the gospels. See Moulton and Geden *Concordance to the Greek Testament* (Edinburgh, 1978) p182.
5. This report is now published as *Blumhardt's Battle* (New York, 1970) translated by Frank S. Boshold. See also Douglas McBain *Eyes That See* (Basingstoke, 1986) p60.
6. ibid p18.
7. ibid p55.
8. ibid p56.
9. ibid p57.
10. James Bentley 'Christoph Blumhardt. Preacher of Hope' in *Theology* **78** (1975) p578. Barth's use of the phrase can be traced in CD IV/3:1 pp168ff. See also William Nicholls *Systematic and Philosophical Theology* (London, 1969) p78.
11. Eberhard Busch *Karl Barth* (London, 1976) p43.
12. Vernard Eller *Thy Kingdom Come: A Blumhardt Reader* (Grand Rapids, 1980) ppxiv–xv.
13. Karl Barth *Theology and the Church* (London, 1962) p55.
14. *Blumhardt's Battle* p9.
15. *New International Dictionary of the Christian Church* (Exeter, 1974) p851.
16. Jessie Penn-Lewis with Evan Roberts *War on the Saints* (New York, 1973). This book was originally published in the 1920s. See also E. Evans *The Welsh Revival of 1904* (London, 1969) pp168–174.

17. Penn-Lewis ibid p96.
18. ibid p54, p96.
19. ibid p221.
20. Lk 10:19.
21. *Pigs in the Parlour* (Kirkwood, 1973) p12.
22. ibid p16.
23. ibid pp113–135.
24. ibid pp123–133.
25. ibid pp57–63.
26. ibid p59,p65.
27. ibid p65.
28. ibid p142.
29. Bill Subritzky *Demons Defeated* (Chichester, 1986) p2.
30. ibid p12.
31. ibid pp37–38.
32. ibid pp67–82,124–126.
33. ibid pp208–209.
34. ibid p212.
35. ibid pp241–251.
36. Eg Don Basham *Deliver Us From Evil* (London, 1972).
37. Particularly worthy of attention are the books by Dr Kurt Koch who was researching this area long before others: *Occult Bondage and Deliverance* (Berghausen, Date not specified); *Christian Counselling and Occultism* (Berghausen, 1972).
38. Don Cupitt *Explorations in Theology* **6** (London, 1979) p50.
39. For the development of this theme see Twelftree *Christ Triumphant* pp135–70; Graham Dow *Churchman* **94** No3 pp199–208.
40. See the international symposium *Demon Possession* (Minneapolis, 1976) John Warwick Montgomery (Ed).
41. Twelftree *op cit* p120.
42. Michael Perry *op cit* p182.
43. *Exorcism. The Findings of a Commission Convened by the Bishop of Exeter* (London, 1972) p23 Dom Robert Petitpierre (Ed).
44. Dr R. K. MacAll 'The Ministry of Deliverance' *Expository Times* **86** (1974–5) p296.
45. Dr M. G. Barker 'Possession and the Occult — A Psychiatrist's View' *Churchman* **94** No 3 (1980) p250.
46. Perry *op cit* p82.
47. Hammond *op cit* p12.
48. ibid p1.
49. Barker *op cit* p250.
50. ibid p251.
51. See further Twelftree *op cit* pp153ff.
52. Jonathan Edwards *The Religious Affections* (London, 1961).
53. In the foreword to E. Evans *The Welsh Revival of 1904* p6.
54. Perry *op cit* p48.

55. L-J. Suenens *Renewal and the Powers of Darkness* (London, 1983) p95.
56. Kurt Koch *Christian Counselling and Occultism* p218.
57. Jay Adams *The Big Umbrella* (Grand Rapids, 1972) p120.
58. Perry *op cit* pp82–97; Petitpierre *Exorcism* pp35–39.

CHAPTER SEVEN

The Lordless Powers

In the previous chapter the focus was upon the phenomenon of demonisation which is evidenced in the lives of individuals. The church of Christ has much to offer those who are entangled and ensnared by demonic powers. At the same time we attempted to indicate the complexity of this issue and to sound cautious notes in view of the tendency to heighten this matter which is to be observed in some quarters. When this is done it serves only to trivialise this area of concern and to make it all the easier to reject. It can be argued for instance that belief in demons is a distinctly unhealthy thing, a symptom of neurotic religion which grows out of an insidious paranoia. Moreover the idea of demons is seen as unhelpful in that it encourages people to avoid responsibility for their own behaviour, giving them opportunity to blame their sins upon an external cause.

The force of all these criticisms needs to be felt. All of them can be seen to be true of certain people at certain times. None of this necessarily invalidates the idea that demonic entities are real, any more than paranoid and neurotic attitudes to Soviet Russia can be held to prove that the Kremlin does not exist or that Marxist-Leninism is a myth. What it does indicate is that the area of the demonic can become a happy hunting ground for people who for some reason or other prefer to live in a fantasy realm rather than the real world. This need not be the case, but unfortunately it sometimes is and such people get spiritual warfare a bad name.

A further mistake needs to be mentioned. It is that of pursuing evil at one level, that is to say of demons, while quite ignoring other dimensions in which the spiritual conflict rages. Indeed, although it is hard to credit the power of darkness with too sophisticated a strategy, since its nature is irrational opposition to the good,[1] it could be said that it suits the power of darkness very well if the attention of Christians is diverted towards occult and demonic concerns and fully absorbed in them, while the wider stage of devilish activity in the political, cultural, national and international spheres is all but ignored. In 1981 trenchant criticisms of the charismatic movement were made along these lines by the Anglo–Catholic Kenneth Leech in his book *The Social God*.[2] He expressed particular concern about the growing preoccupation of 'neo-Pentecostalism' with demonology. He pointed out that in the experience of such people as Dom Robert Petitpierre possession accounted for only one per cent of all cases coming forward in this area and that in the liturgical tradition of the church, exorcism has traditionally been only one part of a 'total liturgy of deliverance and healing in which the realm of evil is rejected and man is restored to the divine realm.'[3] This serves to put exorcism in its place. But Leech's real concern is that the charismatic approach to evil runs the danger of isolating the demonic from the realm of politics which he regards as its true home. By doing this the charismatic renewal distorts the 'demonic symbol' and tends to 'isolate evil within the sphere of the private, and it is this sphere which comes to be seen as par excellence the territory of demons'.[4] He fears that concern with demons will actually divert attention from the real conflict with evil in the world and will therefore effectively lead the church into a complacent support of the status quo rather than being a force for social change. This criticism is one which could be applied to renewal generally which, along with all forms of pietist religion, risks causing people to flee away from engagement with the world into the realm of private ecstatic religious experiences.[5]

Without sharing Leech's apparent scepticism about the reality of the demonic as opposed to its symbolic usefulness, it is possible to agree with the main thrust of his argument. It is true that charismatic renewal could prove to be an escapist reaction against a harsh and God-rejecting world. As a matter of fact it functions in this way in many charismatic churches. The reversal of this process is that charismatic renewal could act as a mighty stimulus for engagement with the world in evangelism, social and political action, providing the spiritual vitality and creativity and the base communities for massive social impact.

In relation to the demonic dimension, it is a matter for specific concern that engagement with afflicted individuals does not so blind our eyes, nor so absorb our attention and energies that we are unable to see and engage the corporate and political activities of the power of darkness. Indeed, we need to be awake to the possibility of diversionary tactics, whereby we become so taken up with a small part of the battle because it is all we can see while the main battle, on a different front, rages without our knowing it.

What is needed is a theology which puts the individual aspects of the demonic into a much broader context and thereby provides the corrective element that is needed in the whole discussion. We require a theological map which will enable us to see the entire battle field and therefore prevent us from being taken unawares. We need to recognise with Walter Wink that 'Satan's heart has always been in international politics' as is evidenced by Revelation 20:3: 'to keep him from deceiving *the nations* any more'.[6]

What is being advocated in this Chapter is that a shift should take place in our understanding. First and foremost we need to perceive the involvement of the power of darkness in the power structures of our world. Only then can we see the individual dimensions of the demonic in their true light. This means that for the great majority of those involved in charismatic renewal a widening of the theological horizons must take place and the fight seen on a broader canvas.

Before attempting to paint the broader picture, it may be helpful to describe how a similar shift from the individual to the political was made in a previous generation. In the last Chapter the experience of Johann Christoph Blumhardt was described. Through his struggle to set a woman free the impetus was given for a renewal movement which came to be centred on a conference centre at Bad Boll of which Blumhardt was the leader. The watchword 'Jesus is Victor!' came to characterise this movement which in some ways parallels the Keswick movement in this country, of which the watchword was and is 'All one in Christ Jesus!' In 1880 the elder Blumhardt died and was succeeded as leader at the centre in Bad Boll by his son Christoph Friedrich Blumhardt (1842–1919), a man who had imbibed and accepted the hopes and experiences of his father. Christoph was renowned as a mass evangelist and healer.[7] But he was to become impatient with what he considered to be the spiritual selfishness of the pious Christians who flocked to Bad Boll.[8] It needs to be understood that both the Blumhardts were in the tradition of Pietism, an evangelical religious movement dating back to the end of the seventeenth century which emphasised, rather like the English Puritans, the place of experience in the Christian life. Doctrine on its own was not enough. What really mattered was life, the experience of salvation. Standing in this tradition, the Blumhardts nonetheless saw the need to reform it. They saw that the danger of Pietism, as with all renewal movements including the present one, was that it could lead to a retreat from the world into egocentric individualism. In place of this they advocated the need for a hope which embraces the whole world. They looked for the coming of the kingdom of God which would make all things new. According to Barth:

> They therefore called the world of piety with its apparently very definite faith in Christ to conversion, to faith in the living Christ who is to come again and make all things new. They gave a central position to the prayer: 'Thy Kingdom come' and 'Even so, come Lord Jesus', and therefore to post-temporal eternity, although this involved them in a conflict with the most earnest representatives of the anthropocentric Christianity of the Post-Reformation period.[9]

The implications of this approach were dramatic. Christoph Blumhardt's interest took a 'turn to the world' and he began to focus upon the socio-economic issues of the day.[10] From 1900–06 he joined the struggle for workers' rights as a Social Democratic deputy in the Stuttgart state parliament, despite the fact that this obliged him to resign his orders as a Lutheran pastor and called down upon him the wrath of civil and ecclesiastical authorities. This action was taken at a time when Social Democracy was strongly Marxist and regarded as extreme. Blumhardt's intention was to bear witness to Christ in the political arena because it was also true there that Jesus was Victor, the bringer of hope. After six years as an influential deputy he then with-drew from the political arena in order to bear witness to the fact that although Christ was Lord even in politics, politics itself did not have the answers to the needs of the world. These were to be found in the kingdom of God. Blumhardt's action is an example of how it is possible to be both involved and responsibly non-involved in the political arena. It was largely out of his witness and thinking that a highly influential movement developed known as Religious Socialism which came to influence profoundly several of the major theologians of the twentieth century and large sections of the European political scene.

The point in relating this story is to indicate how renewal movements are inadequate if they only concern themselves with the inner life of Christians. Sooner or later such move-ments have a tendency to become inward looking unless they engage the world to make a difference in it. The more aware members of such movements, like Blumhardt, begin to feel this and to do something about it. The Blumhardt experience is currently being paralleled within some charis-matic circles. Those who have been involved begin to feel that it is not good enough for the renewing work of the Spirit to be kept in-house, within the church. It needs to flow out from the church into the world.

In recent years there has been a major shift in evangelical thinking away from an isolationist attitude towards the world towards social action and engagement. This is to be entirely welcomed. In the charismatic movement it can currently be perceived that the focus in spiritual warfare is shifting away from the needs of individuals to the needs of society. There is a much greater sense of the need to engage the 'powers' that rule in our society. This can be discerned in the renewed interest in prayer for society, in events such as the 'Make Way' marches which are rooted in the philosophy of 'claiming territory' for the kingdom of

God and in the politicisation which has been taking place
surrounding Christian opposition to government legislation
on Sunday trading laws and the abortion law. It is not the
place here to debate the pros and cons of these particular
issues but to indicate the heightened awareness of the
political dimension in spiritual warfare which is coming to
mark some evangelicals and charismatics. It is good that
this is happening, but if it is to happen in a healthy way
there are two points which need to be watched.

Firstly, it must be seen as of primary importance that in
taking a 'turn to the world' those Christians who feel called
to involve themselves in political action do not become
isolated from their roots in the life of the church. Recent
history reveals significant numbers of people with Christian
backgrounds and commitment who have involved themselves in politics only to find that somewhere along the
road their faith had evaporated. This is not always the case
at all, but where it does happen the reasons are not difficult
to discern. It takes time to sustain any meaningful involvement in the political process. It is possible for church to
get squeezed out. No doubt also, people who become deeply
concerned about the political agenda might be forgiven for
feeling that the churches are somewhat remote from where
the action is. Yet the need to combine spirituality and
political judgement is acute.

Secondly, and more importantly, if the renewal movement in the churches is to affect the surrounding
community, it will only do this in so far as it is able to
develop a political philosophy (for want of a better
expression) which will enable this to happen. Blumhardt
translated his vibrant spiritual experience and hope into a
political position (religious socialism) which was appropriate to the circumstances of his day and enabled him to
apply the message of hope to his society. There was a time
in Britain when Free Church theology went hand in hand

with Liberal politics. Free Church values were given expression in this way politically and the non-conformist conscience made its mark on the community. We need to find a coherent political philosophy, or possibly even several philosophies, which will enable the values for which the church stands to be translated into practical politics. The task of doing this belongs to those who have the ability and training to do it. For this reason it will not be attempted here! But I venture here the tentative suggestion that one piece of the jigsaw puzzle must be an analysis of the way in which the power of darkness interacts with the social structures of human communities.

The church in this world has a mission. It is a mission that is comprised of three parts. The first part is evangelistic. We are called to proclaim the good news of the kingdom of God. This message calls people to repentance and to a new relationship with the God who is Christlike. The second part of the mission concerns social action. We are called to care for people, to heal the sick and love the needy. In doing this we are behaving like Christ, since this is what he did. All Christians are more or less agreed on these parts of the mission, although they may fulfil them in differing ways. The third aspect of the mission is political. It involves living under the Lordship of Christ and this in turn means accepting no other lord, whether this be nation, or wealth or political ruler. Christians live for Christ, and if Caesar asks for what belongs to God, so much the worse for Caesar![11] Christians obey God rather than man.[12] Furthermore, Christ is not only Head of the church but also Head of the universe.[13] All creation must learn to submit to its Lord. To this end Christians are called to exercise a loving witness to the powers of this world.[14]

The recognition that the church plays a political role is now widely made, although not with the degree of unanimity which applies in the case of the evangelistic and social aspects of its mission. Yet here is a problem. Christians who agree on the need for political witness disagree radically as to how this ought to be done. One illustration of this was the fact that in the 1988 presidential elections in the USA, two ordained ministers, Pat Robertson and Jesse Jackson, were among the competitors on opposite sides. Both were rooted in the Christian tradition yet held widely diverging political positions. The essence of the difference between them appeared to be that Robertson stressed personal morality and responsibility while Jackson stressed both the personal and corporate aspects of a moral society. It is the recognition that evil is not simply personal but also structural and corporate that leads to different political positions. Put otherwise, the analysis of what is wrong in society determines the political solutions which are advocated. Where what is discerned is failure in personal responsibility and effort the solution will focus on the individual. Where the emphasis is placed on corrupt and unjust social structures, the emphasis will be on social reform. In reality a true analysis will recognise both personal and corporate dimensions to the problem.

This chapter argues that we should take the social nature of evil seriously without minimising its individual aspects. In this we are in hearty agreement with Andrew Walker: 'It is in the processes and ideologies of the modern world itself that we find the destructive, impersonal and heartless force of the dark Power.'[15] This is not to disagree with the saying of Paul 'our struggle is not against flesh and blood',[16] but rather to say that the form which is taken by the powers of darkness is not that of free floating entities which maraud in the heavenlies and attack individuals. Such powers as exist take form in the very structures of life and seek to do their work by controlling humanity through them. Spiritual warfare cannot be carried on without refer-

139

ence to the actual state of the political, cultural and social context in which we live.

As these statements are of key importance, it is necessary to substantiate them from Scripture. The evidence can be viewed in several ways.

1. The biblical evidence viewed 'concretely'

First of all it can be argued from the life of Jesus that in his conflict with the powers of darkness, that power took form both as individual temptation and attack and as institutional opposition to him. In the life and death of Jesus we therefore see revealed how it is that evil operates in the world. We need to bear in mind that Jesus is the Word of God. It is not simply that he came speaking the Word of God. He was the Word of God. As the Word made flesh he embodied and demonstrated in all his actions the revelation of God to man. In this concrete and particular way, God is revealed to us in history, and in opposition to this Christ we see the nature of evil. Some years ago Professor James Stewart drew attention to what was then a neglected emphasis in New Testament studies, namely the element of spiritual conflict in the life of Jesus.[17] In the cross we see the climax of God's self-revelation in Christ and there are three elements involved in it, the design of man, the will of Jesus and the predestination of God. By the design of man Stewart meant:

a coalition of ascertainable historical forces. It was the human attitudes of pride, self-love and traditionalism and fear which, when worked out into social, political and ecclesiastical magnitudes resulted in the death of the Son of God.[18]

The coalition consisted of religion, politics and popular

opinion. Organised religion was at the cross because it saw itself threatened by Jesus. He was seen as a blasphemer in that he proclaimed and demonstrated the free grace of God towards sinners in a way which overturned the secure, legalistic categories of Jewish religion. He spoke of God's mercy towards the outcast and sinner and embodied this by making friends with the irreligious.[19] This was perceived as a major threat to the religious system and drew out the deep hostility of the conventionally religious to Jesus.

A second member of the coalition was politics. Both Jewish and Roman politics had reason to be displeased with Jesus. He had disappointed the hopes of Jewish nationalism because it seemed at first that he might serve the nationalist purpose.[20] Equally, he had threatened the totalitarian claims of the Roman system because it feared any rival to its own power.[21] From both points of view it was therefore expedient to do away with Jesus. If he had been merely a blasphemer it would have been enough to stone him. Because he was also regarded as a rebel he was actually crucified, the punishment for political offenders.[22]

The third member of the coalition was that of public opinion. The ordinary people, apathetic and easily manoeuvred by the more unscrupulous, are found represented by the crowd at the cross of Christ.[23] This represents the demonic power of mob opinion which can be manipulated in any number of directions according to the occasion. Social forces are found at the cross. Religious, political and social factors are seen in the crucifying of Jesus to rise up against God in opposition. They show themselves to be antichrist. In the life of Jesus the *modus operandi* of the powers of darkness is revealed. They distort and manipulate the fallen structures of human life for their own end. It must therefore be recognised that warfare with Satan must be carried on in the religious, political and social spheres.

2. The biblical evidence viewed 'theologically'

This same point can be argued by reference to the theology of the apostle Paul. Here the focus shifts away from the kind of demonic encounter described in the gospels to the realm of 'principalities and powers'.[24] Despite the demonic struggles which are found in the missionary journeys of Paul,[25] demons hardly figure at all in Paul's letters.[26] This cannot be taken to mean that he did not acknowledge their existence, but it does indicate that he thinks more broadly about the invisible conflict. It is not immediately clear exactly what Paul had in mind when he referred to these powers. There are three broad lines of interpretation.

(a) The first is a view which has been popularised since the war and which argues that Paul had in mind the structures of human existence, that is to say the social, political, cultural and religious forces which invisibly shape human existence. Thus, mythological language is used to describe these realities because it is the only kind of language that gets anywhere near the truth about the invisible world. Paul uses such language to describe his own culture as he experiences it. There is now a large body of literature which argues this position. A short and influential work in this area was produced under the title *Christ and the Powers* by Hendrik Berkhof.[27] Berkhof sought to evaluate the Pauline language which refers on nine occasions to the 'powers'.[28] In addition he sought to make sense of the *stoicheia* (Col 2:8, 20ff), the 'basic principles' (NIV) or 'elemental spirits' (RSV) of the world and sees in all of these ideas expressed by Paul a movement away from notions of personal beings controlling life towards an idea of the 'structures of earthly existence'.[29] Paul, he thinks, is demythologising the ideas of his day concerning supernatural personal powers of good and evil. The 'powers' are the structures of earthly existence which were created by

God (Col 1:16), but are now in a fallen state and are therefore hostile to God (Rom 8:38–39). They behave like tyrants and oppress people because they are not subject to God as Lord. Yet one day they will be restored to their proper function in the consummation.[30] The decisive point for Berkhof is that the New Testament envisages a day when the powers will be reconciled to God and this precludes their being fallen angels.[31]

Berkhof doubts that Paul thought of the powers as personal beings. At most he thought of them as personifications, just as he wrote of sin and death as if they were persons.[32] Others would agree with this judgement. D. E. H. Whiteley states in his standard work on Paul's theology:

> I personally believe that, whatever may be said about the demons of the Synoptics, St Paul, consciously or otherwise, was using mythological language. In other words, there are no principalities or powers, but St Paul employs this language to express something which is both true and important.[33]

The most comprehensive recent study in this area has been done by Walter Wink in his book *Naming the Powers*.[34] After exhaustively examining the New Testament data, Wink concludes that the language of power pervades the whole New Testament, that it is extremely varied, interchangeable and unsystematic but refers consistently to genuine power realities which are heavenly and earthly, divine and human, spiritual and political, invisible and visible, good and evil.[35] Nevertheless, the New Testament language is mythic and needs to be re-examined for today in terms of 'interiority', that is 'inner aspects of material or tangible manifestations of power'. Institutions may be considered to have inner essences and these are the principalities and powers. Likewise, demons are the psychic or spiritual powers emanated by organisations or individuals or 'subaspects of individuals whose energies are bent on overpowering others'.[36]

This is a sophisticated interpretation of the New Testament data which recognises that it is saying something distinctive and authoritative and that this needs to be retranslated into terms which are relevant today. The effect of this is to shift the spiritual battle away from a purely invisible conflict in 'the heavenlies' and into the realm of the social, political, religious and cultural realities of our day.

(b) It might well be imagined that such a process of demythologising has not commanded universal assent. In particular Dr John Stott has taken up the cudgels for a more traditional interpretation of Paul.[37] Dr Stott sees the position taken by Berkhof and others as resulting from embarrassment at the archaic worldview of angels and demons in the New Testament and at the lack of reference to social structures so significant for the modern world. The re-interpreted view of the powers offers us a way of escape from both of these difficulties.[38] He dismisses the 'new' approach as failing to do justice to the spiritual conflict 'in the heavenlies' of which Paul speaks in Ephesians and prefers the traditional interpretation that the 'world rulers of this present darkness' and the 'spiritual hosts of wickedness' of Ephesians 6:12 must be taken as supernatural powers, particularly when the context already specifically refers to the devil (v11,v16).[39] To accept the new interpretation is to overthrow a previously almost universal understanding of what these texts mean. He sees three dangers in the new approach.

Firstly, without reckoning with the reality of the demonic we have no explanation as to why human structures become tyrannical. Secondly, we run the danger of restricting our understanding of the devil's activity if we limit it to the structural. Thirdly, we become too negative towards society and its structures if we see them as being evil. In avoiding the deification of structures we end up demonising them.[40] Having said this, Stott readily acknowledges that supernatural personal agencies can use structures, traditions, institutions and the like for malevolent purposes as media of their ministry.[41]

(c) A third position, and the one advocated here, argues that it is possible to have the best of both worlds and that this is indicated by Scripture itself. We would certainly want to stand with John Stott in affirming the reality of supernatural powers in accordance with the biblical witness. It appears to be irrefutable that this was part of Paul's own understanding, as it was of Jesus. It cannot credibly be argued that Paul did not really believe in the reality of the devil.[42] Rather, Whiteley must be considered correct when he asserts: 'It would seem that St Paul did believe in the real existence of a "personal" Satan and probably of other personal demons'.[43] The question here is whether we feel obliged to accept the teaching at its face value or whether we wish to demythologise it and give it another form. However, while agreeing with Stott at this point, there appears to be no reason why the language of the powers could not also be taken to refer to the structures of human existence. This would appear to be warranted for the following reasons.

Firstly, there is clearly an ambiguity in Paul's language such that certain references could be taken either to refer to earthly or to spiritual powers. Michael Green writes: 'The truth of the matter is that words like principalities, powers and thrones are used both of human rulers and of the spiritual forces which lie behind them.'[44] He concludes that there is a deliberate ambiguity which is particularly evident in 1 Corinthians 2:8: 'None of the rulers of this age understood it, for if they had, they would not have crucified the Lord of glory.' Green stresses the need 'to realise the flexibility of such terms as principalities and powers in the usage of the New Testament. They do, on occasion, refer to human authorities. They do, for the main part, refer to superhuman agencies in the spiritual world.'[45] The ambiguity of the language is also recognised in Wink's study of the subject in which he argues that it is deliberately fluid and is used to comprehend spiritual and political, invisible and structural realities.[46] This is further confirmed by Markus Barth who comments: 'The principalities and powers are at the same time intangible spiritual entities and concrete historical, social or psychic structures or institutions of all created things and all created life.'[47]

We are not obliged to agree with Dr Stott therefore that the New Testament has nothing to say about social structures, or that the position outlined here represents an 'uneasy compromise'.[48] The point is precisely that the power structures of human life are vulnerable and open to invasion by the powers of darkness. It is largely through these that they exercise their hold. In view of Stott's acknowledgement of this fact as an empirical reality it appears that the only issue at stake here is whether this reality is spoken of in Paul's theology or whether it is being read back in from our own perspective. He seems to deny that it is envisaged in Scripture while accepting its reality in actual experience. The argument here is that what is part of our total human experience, namely that the power structures of society interact with the powers of darkness to create enslavement and exploitation, is actually quite in accord with the ambiguous way in which power language is used in the New Testament. This very ambiguity suggests an openness of the fallen power systems of human society to demonic and Satanic influence.

If this genuinely accords with the teaching of Paul it can be seen that there is no contradiction between his theology and the concrete experience of Jesus. Indeed, Paul is simply explicating what is visible in the life of Christ. As the powers of religion, politics and popular opinion were used to crucify the Son of God and the power of darkness takes form in these powers, so Paul speaks of the powers and principalities which threaten human life. He makes explicit what is to be perceived in the life of Jesus. He is using words to expound the Word. Just as his doctrine of justification by faith can be seen as explaining in theological terms the actions of Jesus in befriending sinners, so it is with the powers. He expounds the actual experience of Jesus in his encounter with evil, an experience which is repeated in the life of the church. We may not agree with the 'new interpretation' of the powers in demythologising the devil, but we can see how these insights can augment our understanding of how it is that the powers of darkness work. As Green puts it:

> Inflation and unemployment, the arms race and the corruption of morals, these are all manifestations in the modern state of principalities and powers. The state does not want these things, for the most part. It struggles hard to get rid of them. But it fails. It is in the grip of a power beyond its own.[49]

This is not to demonise structures but simply to recognise that such structures can enhance or distort human existence according to the power that is at work within them.

3. The biblical evidence viewed 'apocalyptically'

A third cross-sectional view of this reality is to be found in the apocalyptic imagery of the Book of Revelation, particularly chapters 12–13. Here we see an unholy triad ranged against God and his people in the form of the dragon (Rev 12:3), the beast out of the sea (Rev 13:1) and the beast out of the earth (Rev 13:12). The dragon represents Satan as is clear from verse 19, the beast out of the sea is the power of Rome which blasphemously claims supremacy. The beast out of the earth represents the religious system of the Empire which is devoted to the worship of the Emperor (Rev 13:12). Behind the whole system of totalitarian power and false religion is the manipulative power of evil (Rev 13:2). In this chapter, 'the struggle of the saints against the Caesars is portrayed in the context of an age-long resistance to the God of heaven on the part of evil powers'.[50] The evil power takes form here in the political and religious structures of the Roman Empire. The opposition to God's people is shown in a combination of political and ideological hostility. This does not mean that the state is intrinsically evil. According to Romans 12:4 it is 'God's servant for your good'. It does mean that at certain times and places the state has become demonised and indeed, that it is always in danger of doing so if it goes beyond its proper function of serving mankind. In some countries, the totalitarian perversion of the state is obvious. In others it is concealed but will be brought out the moment the vested interests of the powerful are threatened.

Although expressed apocalyptically, that is in symbolic and to us lurid terms, the picture which emerges here is in line with that already discerned in the more theological statements of Paul and the more concrete circumstances of Jesus' life. The picture which emerges from all three cross-sectional views is of a world in which the invisible realities which determine and shape life can be seen to consist of spiritual and structural powers. The structures reflect and participate in the fallen state of the human race. They are vulnerable to invasion by spiritual powers. They reflect the sinfulness of mankind and compound the total human problem. Yet they are not intrinsically evil. Having been made by God they will one day be redeemed and will resume their proper function (Col 1:15–20). In the meantime they can be humanised and brought back into line in order to serve and not oppress. The powers that at the moment operate as if they were a law unto themselves need to be helped to see that they too have a Lord. They can no longer function as if they were lordless powers. It is here that our corporate warfare needs to be recognised.

As an illustration of this we highlight one issue. There is the insidious danger of nationalism. It is natural for people to love their country and to appreciate its strengths. But the perversion of a proper love of country is nationalism, whereby the nation's interests assume a god-like status. When this happens we are in danger of being controlled by a power which has become demonic. This is all the more threatening when nationalism seeks to harness religion to its own ends. This was abundantly clear when Hitler attempted to domesticate the church in the interests of National Socialism. The same trend can be discerned in the USA where Christianity and Americanism are closely identified. Christianity is in danger of losing its power by being harnessed to the interests of the nation, perpetuating a myth of American purity and righteousness. Prosperity teaching baptises America's success values into the faith and so the Bible is used to bolster up materialism and greed.

At no point was this identification of Christianity and Americanism more clearly visible than in the Congressional hearings surrounding Lt-Col Oliver North. North, a charis-matic Christian, was shocked to the core when accused of irregularity in his private life. But he proudly confessed to being ready to lie, deceive, kill and maim in the name and for the sake of America. The interests of America and of the Christian cause were clearly to be identified. What would be unthinkable to him in one sphere was perfectly possible in another. It is obvious that this is a distorted perspective. When such a thing happens, Christians should take warning. There is a beguiling, deceptive power at work which has the ability to ensnare Christians and make them prisoners of their nation, their social class, or their group interest.

Until and unless Christians perceive this and resolve not to be conformed to the world but to be transformed, radically renewed in the image of Christ, they are fooling themselves that they are engaged in spiritual warfare. Indeed outrage at the rise of the occult, prayer marches and attempts to bind the powers of darkness could all be one major deception and diversion if we fail to appreciate the subtlety of the issues at stake. While believing self-righteously that we are living for God in one area we could in fact be selling out completely in another. The key to all of this is our ability to recognise the form that evil can take in the world's corporate structures and the difficulty we have in recognising it because we just cannot see it. This requires understanding and perception on our part and the ability to think as well as pray.

Unless we recognise the dual aspect of the powers, the spiritual and the structural, we may miss the point. The solution does not lie in prayer alone. We must see the way in which the power of darkness interacts with and draws strength from the investment that fallen people and struc-tures make in it. It is not only that there are spiritual forces which need to be ejected from the structure. There are powerful structures which compound the strength of the power of darkness. The two are symbiotic. If we use the weapon of prayer to confound the power of darkness, it simply reappears again unless we deal with a major source of its energy in the matrix of fallen human life. Here we are expressing again the idea that the power of darkness actually grows and increases to the extent to which 'faith' is given to it.

Spiritual warfare must therefore be carried on simultaneously on two fronts, through prayer and through persuasive action. In prayer the power of the kingdom of God is given access to human life. In persuasive action men and women and institutions are persuaded to invest in what is good and true rather than what is wrong and false. These two things together constitute our spiritual warfare as we take seriously the spiritual dimension of the human dilemma and the structural forms and distortions which are produced by the world, the flesh and the devil in coalition. In the final chapter we will attempt to describe the sort of church that is needed to fulfil this task.

REFERENCES

1. On this see A. Walker *Enemy Territory* p35: 'Evil may have intelligence, but the Devil's strategies against the church are not, it seems to me, to be understood as rational military strategies, rather they are more like desperate and increasingly vicious attacks.'
2. Kenneth Leech *The Social God* (London, 1981).
3. ibid pp91–2.
4. ibid p94.
5. ibid pp95–6.
6. Wink *Unmasking the Powers* p39.
7. V. Eller *Thy Kingdom Come: A Blumhardt Reader* pxix.
8. James Bentley 'Christopher Blumhardt. Preacher of Hope' in *Theology* **78** (1975).

9. Barth CD II/1 p633.
10. Eller *op cit* pxx.
11. Mt 22:21.
12. Acts 5:29.
13. Eph 1:20–3; 4:15.
14. Eph 3:10–11.
15. Walker *op cit* p64.
16. Eph 6:12.
17. James S. Stewart 'On a neglected emphasis in NT Theology' *Scottish Journal of Theology* 4 (1951) pp292–301.
18. ibid p295.
19. Mt 11:19. See also Jürgen Moltmann *The Crucified God* (London, 1974) pp128–135.
20. Jn 6:15.
21. Lk 23:2; Mt 27:37; Acts 17:7.
22. Moltmann *op cit* p136.
23. Mk 15:13–14.
24. Eph 6:12.
25. Acts 16:16–18; 19:11–16.
26. There are the references in 1 Cor 10:20f, but the point is substantially true.
27. H. Berkhof *Christ and the Powers* (Scottdale, 1962).
28. Rom 8:38f; 1 Cor 2:8; 1 Cor 15:24–6; Eph 1:20f; 2:1f; 3:10; 6:12; Col 1:16; 2:15.
29. Berkhof *op cit* p23.
30. ibid p66.
31. ibid p25. Compare the 'all things' of Col 1:16 with the 'all things' of 1:20.
32. ibid p24.
33. Whiteley *The Theology of St Paul* p20. See also p29.
34. Wink *Naming the Powers* (Philadelphia, 1984).
35. ibid pp99–102.
36. ibid pp104–105.
37. Stott *God's New Society* (Leicester, 1979) pp260–287. *The Cross of Christ* (Leicester, 1986) p233.
38. *God's New Society* p271.
39. ibid pp272–273.
40. ibid p274.
41. ibid.
42. As is argued by Leech *op cit* p90.
43. Whiteley *op cit* p29. See 2 Cor 6:15; Eph 4:27; 6:11.
44. Green *I Believe in Satan's Downfall* p84. In reference to men he cites Lk 12:11 and Acts 4:26 and to superhuman powers Col 1:16; 2:15; Rom 8:38; Eph 6:12.
45. ibid p86.
46. Wink *Naming the Powers* p100.
47. M. Barth *Ephesians 4–6; The Anchor Bible* (New York, 1976) p800.

48. Stott *op cit* p271.
49. Green *op cit* p49.
50. G. R. Beasley-Murray *The Book of Revelation* (London, 1974) p191.

CHAPTER EIGHT

The Dedemonising of Creation

The task we are about to attempt should probably have been accomplished before now. We are concerned to show how the power of darkness has been overcome in Jesus Christ. It may well be that this chapter should have been the first to have been written. After all, we have been keen to demonstrate that the power of darkness must be kept in its place. The concern has been to develop a way of thinking about evil which takes it seriously but does not let it get out of hand. The power of darkness is deceptive and is keen to convince us that it is overwhelming, all pervading and worthy of our attention. What better way would there have been to counteract this than to show from the very beginning that its power is a negated power, an enemy which has been overcome in Christ? For the Christian, the mere thought of the power of darkness should be immediately accompanied by the knowledge that it has met its match and been trodden under foot by Jesus.

The fact that we have chosen to delay consideration of how Christ has gained the victory until now is purely a question of method. Is it better to outline the problem before dealing with the solution or to do it the other way round? In favour of the former approach, focusing on the negative before accentuating the positive, it might be said that to know the size of the problem is helpful in that it enables us to appreciate the solution when it comes. First the bad news, then the good news. On the other hand, to begin by affirming the victory of Christ over evil means that any subsequent investigation of the nature and activity of evil is bathed in the light of that victory. From the outset, therefore, the power of darkness is seen in true perspective and kept firmly where it belongs in our thoughts, under the heel of the Victor!

As it happens we have chosen to move from the negative to the positive, but have attempted from the start to show that the defeat of evil by Christ undergirds our entire investigation. The task now is to consider how the victory was gained and how it may be held to alter the circumstances of the world in which we live.

Earlier we commented on the origin of the slogan 'Jesus is Victor!' in the experience of the elder Blumhardt. The New Testament presents us with the picture of a triumphant Christ, one who through humiliation and suffering did what was necessary to destroy the power of evil. To illustrate this we need to refer to various strands of the New Testament witness where the point is made abundantly clear.

In the *synoptic strand* we find the reference of Jesus to binding the strong man in order that his possessions may be plundered and carried off (Mt 12:29). This verse occurs in the context of Jesus' healing of the demon possessed. He is accused by the Pharisees of doing so by the power of Beelzebub, the prince of demons (v24). Jesus' reply is to the effect that he drives out Satan by the Spirit of God and this is the sign that the kingdom of God has begun to come. The point of the parable is that there is one who is stronger than the strong man, namely the Holy Spirit by whose power at work in Jesus the demons are expelled.[1]

The Johannine strand reflects a similar understanding of the work of Christ but sees the defeat of evil being accomplished in the cross. 'Now is the time for judgement on this world; now the prince of this world will be driven out. But I, when I am lifted up from the earth, will draw all men to myself' (Jn 12:31–32). The train of thought here is that the world's situation is changed by the lifting up of Jesus Christ on the cross. The dethroning of Satan is accompanied by the enthroning of Christ over the world he died to save.[2] In this saying of Jesus there are echoes of Luke 10:18: 'I saw Satan fall like lightning from heaven', and of course 1 John 3:8: 'The reason the Son of God appeared was to destroy the devil's work.'

The *Pauline strand* is well represented by Colossians 2:9–15 where the work of Christ is portrayed as a clear victory over the powers and authorities. Christ is the head of every power and authority (2:10). Having died on the cross he has cancelled the legal record of our sins that 'was against us and stood opposed to us' (v14). Moreover he has 'disarmed the powers and authorities' and 'has made a public spectacle of them, triumphing over them by the cross' (v15). Paul moves from forgiveness of sins to the victory of the cross since it is through the guilt of men and women that the dark powers are able to hold them in their power. Once this guilt is removed by atonement, the hold of the powers over mankind is broken. The picture painted in these verses is of a victory parade in which the conquered powers are drawn along in God's triumphal procession and paraded as enemies who have been overcome and whose rule is now over. They must now serve the Victor. They may continue to exist and may still be hostile. They are unwilling servants of Christ, but they have been overcome and their ultimate overthrow is sure and certain although still future.[3]

The *Petrine strand* of testimony may be discerned most

clearly in 1 Peter 3:18–22 which again brings together the work of Christ on the cross and the victory he now enjoys. Christ has 'died for sins once for all'. He has been 'put to death in the body but made alive by the Spirit' (v18). He has proclaimed his victory to the imprisoned spirits (v19) and is now in heaven at God's right hand 'with angels, authorities and powers in submission to him' (v22). Here the victory of Christ is seen as being achieved in his resurrection through which he has been raised above the spiritual powers which opposed him. In this way the evil powers have been shattered.[4]

The final testimony to which we refer is that of the *apocalyptic strand* and particularly to the highly coloured vision of Revelation 12. In this we see a scene of conflict. The dragon persecutes from his birth the Messiah who is born of the messianic people but God raises him to his very throne (v5). The dragon here represents the devil working through the power of the Roman Empire (compare v7 with v3). Michael and his angels (representing the forces of God) fight against the dragon who is hurled down with his angels to the earth. But the conquest of the devil is made possible 'by the blood of the Lamb and the word of their testimony' (v4). In other words, 'it is the redemptive death and resurrection of the Christ confessed in the gospel (the "testimony") which has conquered the devil'.[5] Here in the apocalyptic language of the Revelation is clear testimony to the victory of Christ. The victory has been gained through the blood of Christ. In Revelation 5 this is strikingly illustrated in John's vision of God. The only one found worthy to open the scroll of human destiny is the Lion of Judah.

Do not weep! See, the Lion of the tribe of Judah, the Root of David, has triumphed. He is able to open the

scroll and its seven seals. Then I saw a Lamb, looking
as if it had been slain... (Rev 5:5–6).

The Lion of Judah is also the Lamb of God. It is through
his sacrificial work as the Lamb of God who takes away
the sins of the world that Jesus Christ has become the
victorious Lion of Judah.

We could go on amassing the biblical evidence to demonstrate the way the work of Christ is portrayed as victory
over hostile powers but the case is sufficiently proved. The
unequivocal testimony is that Jesus is Victor.

In view of this, Christian theology has made much use
of the idea of victory in describing the work of Christ.
Over fifty years ago a book was published by the Swedish
theologian Gustav Aulen (1879–1977) which sought to
recapture the concept of atonement as victory. He argued
that recent thought had sought to understand atonement
either through the 'satisfaction' approach associated with
the name of Anselm or through the 'subjective' approach
associated with Abelard. One saw Christ's work as
satisfying God's honour (or his wrath in another version).
The other understood it in terms of its ability to influence
sinners towards the good. In preference, Aulen advocated
the renewal of the concept of victory to explain the cross.

Christ — Christus Victor — fights against and triumphs
over the evil powers of the world, the 'tyrants' under
which mankind is in bondage, and in Him God
reconciles the world to Himself.[6]

He describes this as the 'classic idea' and the 'dramatic
view' of the atonement[7] which has fallen into neglect in
Christian thinking despite being the fundamental motif for
understanding the work of Christ. Its strength is that it
very definitely sees atonement as God's work and therefore

avoids the man-centred or legalistic approaches of the other theories. It is the characteristic teaching of the New Testament,[8] of the early church fathers, especially of Irenaeus,[9] and of Martin Luther. Luther argued that mankind was imprisoned by the tyrants of sin, death, the devil, wrath and the law and that Christ overcame them all.[10] He saw the work of Christ as one of deliverance brought about by God in the drama of the death and resurrection of Christ.

Aulen's thesis has been criticised from a number of angles but is basically sound. He might be faulted for implying that the classical idea excludes any other description or is to be preferred above them. In fact, if Christ has won a victory on the cross it must be because he made an atonement there which propitiated the wrath of God and expiated the sin of man. As Paul Althaus has written:

> The satisfaction which God's righteousness demands constitutes the primary and decisive significance of Christ's work and particularly of his death. Everything else depends on this satisfaction, including the destruction of the might and authority of the demonic powers.[11]

Despite this qualification Aulen is accurate in stressing the dramatic context in which the atoning work of the cross is set and of which it is the decisive moment. It is by the blood of Christ poured out for sinners that guilt is removed and bondage broken. It is to announce and reveal this breaking of Satan's power, this finished work, that Christ is raised from the dead and enthroned as king over all.

The retelling of this drama and conquest is the concern of the church. Indeed it is with this story that the whole Bible is concerned. John Stott sees six stages in this drama. It is predicted in the Old Testament. It is begun in the ministry of Jesus as demons are dismissed, sicknesses healed and disordered nature acknowledges its Lord. It is achieved at the cross where the prince of this world is driven out. It is confirmed and announced in the resurrection when the victory of the cross was endorsed, proclaimed and demonstrated. It is extended as the church preaches Christ in the power of the Holy Spirit. It will be consummated when Christ returns and makes his victory universal and total.[12] From this perspective of an accomplished work, the Christian views and considers the still active power of darkness. Though active its days are numbered and its doom sealed.

There are other ways in which we may recount the story. The gospel is fundamentally simple. It recounts a pattern of creation, fall, redemption, extension and consummation. Within this context we may understand the history and future of the human race and of those powers and principalities which although invisible are strikingly real.

1. Creation

According to Colossians 1:16 through Christ 'all things were created: things in heaven and on earth, visible and invisible, whether thrones or powers, rulers or authorities; all things were created by him or for him'. Whatever we understand by powers and principalities and however we explain the disorder which now marks them, we cannot escape the fact that they are created realities. They have come into being through the creative work of God in Christ without whom 'nothing was made that has been made' (Jn 1:3). In Romans 8:38 the powers are numbered among created things. But they are created realities which owe their origin to God along with the rest of creation. When we speak of the devil we remember that whatever the devil is, he does not and cannot exist independently of the God who created all. Even he must trace his origin to the

Creator. We live in a world that has come from God and exists because of his decision to let things be.

2. Fall

Colossians 1:19–20 goes on to speak of the day when all things will be reconciled to God. Implicit in this passage therefore is an event or a series of events to which the Bible refers only obliquely. Somehow and at sometime after the creation, the invisible powers and principalities have become estranged from God leaving them in a condition requiring them to be reconciled or pacified (vv19–20). Here, as indeed in all the Bible, 'a cosmic rupture of enormous proportions' is implied.[13] A fall of man is elsewhere plainly spoken of.[14] The idea of a pre-human cosmic fall, a massive aberration in the created world of unseen reality introducing a great disorder, is only gently hinted at. Jude 6 and 2 Peter 2:4 point in this direction, even though faintly. Colossians 2:15 speaks of the need for powers and authorities to be disarmed and implies a cosmic conflict which takes place in an invisible realm. It is clear that something has happened to bring this about. In view of previous discussions concerning the lordless powers in which we have argued that New Testament terms are fluid and include the spiritual and the structural we need to conceive of this disruption in three stages.

(i) The first is that which we have described as an 'angelic catastrophe'. In describing this transcendent realm we are forced to use symbolic, even 'mythological' language. But we are describing something that has actually happened. It is in the area of 'the devil and his angels'[15] that we must look for an explanation of where and how the great disorder of creation originates.

(ii) The second stage of the cosmic rupture involves the

wilful disobedience of mankind in which men and women have given themselves, and still do, to siding with the dark power. This is unmistakably the message of Genesis 3. The devil

is not impersonal like stones or bureaucracies: he is a non-person. The Devil has become all that God is not; he is not beyond personality — he is without it. His purpose in creation is not to destroy God; he knows that he cannot do that. He wants to draw us into the vortex of non-personhood that he has become, and the nothing-ness of non-being that he is becoming. Satan, in short, aims to take as many of us with him as he can.[16]

By gaining access to the human race the power of dark-ness has greatly increased its own power since now it may feed parasitically on estranged human life, bloating itself on the lifeblood that it sucks out. It thrives on the attention it receives and magnifies itself. And this is not all.

(iii) The third stage in the drama of disruption involves the fall in and with the human race of those created elements of human life which were intended to give shape and order to human society. As man has emancipated himself from God, so his own possibilities now emancipate themselves from him. Thinking that he is lord over his own life he is actually the prisoner of created forces which have become disorderly. The powers which we have already referred to as social, political, religious and cultural begin to dominate mankind. It is difficult to avoid speaking of these powers in language other than the personal even though they are not. Paul says that there are many gods and many lords which paradoxically are nothing.[17] Yet they claim mankind's allegiance. Jesus warned of the god of money which he called Mammon.[18] It rivalled the true God. No doubt Jesus never thought that there actually was a god called Mammon, but he recognised the almost personal way in which money claimed loyalty and pushed people in an unrighteous direction.[19] The use of personalised imagery here perhaps indicates that behind the forces which determine existence are the powers of the devil and his angels who are in some way personal.

In some of his last work Karl Barth was to write of the powers which have fallen in and with mankind.[20] He describes how in Goethe's poem *The Sorcerer's Apprentice* human capacities become spirits with a life of their own and sees in this an illustration of how mankind's own possibilities take on their own momentum and become the motors of society. If mankind slips out of God's service:

> he thereby forfeits the lordship that should be his. In the sudden or gradual movement with which man breaks free from God, he revolutionizes the natural forces that are coordinated with him. . . It is he who is at the helm, who pulls the levers, who presses the knobs. Nevertheless, they automatically and autonomously rumble and work and roll and roar and clatter outside him, without him, past him and over him. He finds that he himself is subject to their law which he has foreseen, and to their power, which he has released. Turning aside from God, he is himself displaced, that is, jerked out of his proper position in relation to these forces into one that is unworthy of him. Still his slaves, they now confront him as robots which he himself has to serve, and not without being forced to fear their possible pranks.[21]

Here then is a description of the fall which has produced the great disorder which now bedevils us. It can clearly be seen to consist of those three enemies which are familiar to the Christian church—the devil, the flesh and the world.

3. Redemption

The redeeming work of Christ needs to take account of the problem that we have just described. It must provide the solution to the fall in its three stages or dimensions of the devil, the flesh and the world. For the sake of clarity we shall consider how Christ has overcome each of the enemies, taking them in reverse order.

(a) Overcoming the world. 'Take heart! I have overcome the world', said Jesus (Jn 16:33). It must be admitted that this seemed a strange thing to say and a strange time to say it! Jesus was on the verge of being crucified, how then could he be said to have overcome the world? Yet we are faced with the fact that the apparent defeat of the cross is portrayed as a victory. What kind of victory is this? It is the victory of a man who, unlike all other men and women, refuses to be dominated by the powers which have been let loose in the world through the fall and which now control mankind. He acknowledges the Father's authority above and beyond them. The idolatrous concerns of worldly power, legalistic religion and human popularity are unable to dominate Jesus. In the temptation narrative described in Luke 4:1–12, Satan offers Jesus the possibility of worldly success and influence and this is equivalent to worshipping Satan (v9). But Jesus resists Satan and overcomes him. He lives in obedience to God and rejects idolatry: that is, making someone or something other than God his ultimate concern. He does in the wilderness what Adam failed to do in the garden. In doing this Jesus breaks the dominion of the world. He breaches the dyke of human conformity and disobedience. In this light, the cross of Christ may be seen to be the ultimate act of refusal to conform. Even though his life is taken he refuses to leave off from the way of obedience to God.

Only in a very restricted sense is it right to understand the cross as submission — as a man's free submission to the dark powers that would destroy him. The submission is depicted, for example, in the Fourth Gospel, as an active exercise of authority: it is a submission that consists in the refusal to submit.[22]

In this way, Christ opens up for the whole of humanity the possibility of a life free from the domination of the world and its powers. We are able to live as free men and women.

(b) Overcoming the flesh. 'For Christ died for sins once for all, the righteous for the unrighteous, to bring you to God' (1 Pet 3:18). When we speak of Christ's death for the human race we are speaking of the crucial and pivotal moment in the work of redemption. Christ died in place of and for the sake of men and women. He bore their sins in such a way as to be 'the Lamb of God who takes away the sin of the world' (Jn 1:29). In this way God himself provides the means whereby wrath may be propitiated and sin expiated. The sacrifice of Christ is effective in its Godward dimension in dealing with the holy wrath of God which threatens us and in its manward dimension in atoning for guilt and removing the very thing that alienates us from God. Now that guilt has been atoned for the possibility of being reconciled to God is produced. By the work of the Spirit this becomes a reality. It means that people can be changed from within, overcoming the compulsive drives of sin, crucifying the old downward drag of our distorted natures and creating the possibility of holy living in the energy which God gives. The message of the cross of Christ may therefore be seen as having the power of God for salvation. It releases into us the power which judges our old life and opens up a new one. The flesh is therefore overcome.

(c) Overcoming the devil. 'Now the prince of this world will be driven out' (Jn 12:31). The cross of Christ has removed the source of the devil's domination of the human race. It is because mankind is alienated from God and guilty before him that the power of darkness has sway over them. Once guilt has been atoned for there is no longer any reason why Satan should accuse and oppress human beings. This very fact is accomplished in the cross, resurrection and ascension of Christ which sees him lifted up above the earth and then above every power and authority. At God's right hand Christ has supreme authority and is ruling over the processes of time and history until 'he has put all his enemies under his feet' (1 Cor 15:25).

According to these verses, God is heavily into *peristroika*, restructuring! The events of cross and resurrection speak of a fundamental alteration in the spiritual conflict whereby Christ has conquered the power of the devil, the sin of man and the alienated structures of the world. It is this victory which is the cause of Christian confidence when faced with the continuing reality of the power of darkness.

4. Extension

All that we have already said brings us up to date. We are currently living in the time which follows the victory of Christ and which precedes the moment of final victory. It is for this reason that the spiritual conflict appears to be more intense than ever. In the language of the Book of Revelation, the devil has been cast down from heaven to earth and the battle is at its fiercest (Rev 12:12). The fact that evil is very active is not a sign that its power has not been conquered but that having been vanquished it knows

167

that its time is short and therefore is engaged in intense struggle.

In the period of extension, the task of the church is to see the kingdom of God which came in, and with Jesus, spreading throughout the world. The kingdom of God will be seen in the casting out of Satan (Lk 11:20), the rescuing of people from sin and guilt (Col 1:13), and in the humanizing of human society so that it may serve God and man in the orderly fashion which is its proper function (Eph 1:20–21; Phil 2:10–11; 1 Cor 15:24–25). We cannot pretend that any of this is easy. The language of conflict and warfare often seems appropriate to this struggle. According to Paul, 'We must go through many hardships to enter the kingdom of God' (Acts 14:22). There are struggles with the devil, the world and the flesh and none of them is easy. There is no room for triumphalism, the easy celebration of victory or superiority. But there is room for, and a need of, the underlying sense of confidence and triumph, of a victory which has already been won and which will one day be complete, to sustain us in the task.

One of the crucial things that Christians need to grasp in the period of the extension of the kingdom of God, is a proper sense of the 'even now' and the 'not yet'. The kingdom has come and is among us, therefore we may expect evidence of its presence and power. It is present as a dynamic force which means that tomorrow has already broken into today. We have a foretaste of what is to be and signs of the coming reality. Still, the kingdom is not yet. It is not fully come and manifest. We will therefore only know in part or possess in part. We will have enough now to sustain us, but not enough completely to satisfy us or leave us feeling there is nothing more to hope for. Christian existence is peculiar in that it is caught between here and there, present and future, strength and weakness, success and failure, cross and resurrection. When we are tempted to despair we need to remember that it was not in spite of, but *through* Gethsemane and Golgotha that the world's redemption was achieved. Christians too are called to share in Christ's sufferings for the world and to await the day of resurrection.

5. Consummation

But the day will come. The morning will dawn and the sun of righteousness will rise with healing in its wings. The whole Bible points towards the day when God will be supreme in his world.

The Jewish people have always found it difficult to accept that Jesus is the Messiah. One reason is the fact that in their interpretation, when the Messiah comes he comes to put things right, to bring in the age of justice and mercy and to abolish the darkness. Christ came, but the darkness continues. How then can he be the Messiah? Some Jews at the time of Jesus attempted to interpret the diverse Old Testament passages which referred to the coming of Messiah by teaching that two Messiahs would come. One would be a suffering Messiah, fulfilling the servant songs recorded in Isaiah. The other would be a great king who would come and rule, fulfilling the expectation of a Davidic king (Ezek 37:18–28). Christians do not believe in two Messiahs who come once, but in one Messiah who comes twice. Christ came as the Lamb to atone. He will come again as the Lion to complete and to consummate the work he has already achieved. Having reordered and recreated in his first coming he is now by the Spirit transforming the world until it is brought into complete and universal harmony (Eph 1:9–10; Col 2:19–20). It is to this day that Christians see the whole world moving, not smoothly as if in a steady and measurable progression but through the conflict and struggle that belong to the present age.

The point of this chapter is to underline the fact that the power of darkness has been put in its place by Jesus Christ. Although it enjoys a measure of vitality, it is comprehended and controlled by God who is working out his purpose. Gustav Aulen completed his classic work on the atonement with the words:

> For my own part, I am persuaded that no form of Christian teaching has any future before it except such as can keep steadily in view the reality of the evil in the world, and go to meet it with the battle-song of triumph.[23]

Because of the dedemonising of the world by Christ, the breaking of the power of darkness, we are able to do just this in anticipation of the day when all the world shall be free at last.

REFERENCES

1. Floyd V. Filson *The Gospel according to St Matthew* (London, 1971) p150.
2. G. R. Beasley-Murray *Word Biblical Commentary 36: John* (Waco, 1987) p214.
3. Peter O'Brien *Word Biblical Commentary 44: Colossians, Philemon* (Waco, 1982) p129.
4. J. N. D. Kelly *The Epistles of Peter and Jude* (London, 1969) p163.
5. G. R. Beasley-Murray *The Book of Revelation* (London, 174) p196.
6. Gustav Aulen *Christus Victor* (London, 1931) p20.
7. ibid pp20–21.
8. ibid pp83ff.
9. ibid pp32ff.
10. ibid p124.
11. Paul Althaus *The Theology of Martin Luther* (Philadelphia, 1966) p220.
12. Stott *The Cross of Christ* pp231–239.

13. Peter O'Brien 'Principalities and Powers: Opponents of the Church' in D. A. Carson *Biblical Interpretation and the Church* (Exeter, 1984) p138.
14. Gen 3; Rom 5:12–21.
15. Rev 12:7–9.
16. Walker *Enemy Territory* p34.
17. 1 Cor 8:5.
18. Mt 6:24; Lk 16:13.
19. Lk 16:11 (RSV).
20. Karl Barth *The Christian Life. Dogmatics Vol IV Part 4* (Edinburgh, 1981) p228. The Chapter headings 'The Lordless Powers' and 'The Dedemonizing of Creation' are inspired by this section, pp213–232.
21. ibid p216.
22. Colin Gunton 'Christus Victor Revisited' *Journal of Theological Studies* **35** (April 1985) p142.
23. Aulen *op cit* p176.

CHAPTER NINE

The Love of Power and the Power of Love

Because we are in a spiritual battle the language of military conflict is appropriate. The Son of God came to destroy the works of the devil. The Church of God is wrestling with the opposing forces of darkness. We are to put on the armour of God. The Book of Revelation describes war in heaven. The world is moving towards the final spiritual conflict in the last battle called Armageddon. Besides these New Testament references, the language of conflict comes easily to those who are acquainted with the many battles of the Old Testament and the picture of God as a warrior. The language of war helps us to describe our Christian experience. We fight against temptations, trial, difficulties and against the evil which is within us and beyond us. Few Christians can have escaped the poignant sense of needing to 'win through' and to overcome the obstacles which are placed in the way. From these facts we conclude that warfare language has a useful and indeed necessary part to play.

Battle imagery has been making a comeback in the church's vocabulary. It is common to sing songs about being the army of the Lord, taking the land, possessing the fruit, wielding the sword. We are ready to bind the enemy, to trample on the devil, to call the powers to bow down. The clenched fist, as well as the open upraised hand, has become a sign of the charismatic church. The raised voice, authoritative command and the aggressive posture towards an invisible enemy is now part of our stock in trade.

Once Christians were the 'quiet in the land' who kept a low profile, busied themselves with their own affairs and endeavoured as far as they could to live peacefully with all. Unfortunately, this attitude also meant that they were inclined to be conformist and to allow evil to triumph while good men did nothing. The evangelical withdrawal from political and social engagement, which has more recently been seen as a major fault, was a direct outgrowth of the view that the root of all problems was the need for individual transformation. More recently we have been inclined to see that the changing of the individual must be accompanied by the transformation of the social context if we are to do justice to the gospel of the *kingdom* rather than simply one of personal salvation. Indeed the mood has now so changed that Christians are on the move politically and have geared themselves up to enter the political fray. They see the moral chaos which threatens to engulf the streets of our communities.

I recall a pivotal moment in this change of mood. It was after the upheavals of the 1960s which were marked by riots, strikes, sit-ins and demonstrations. It was a response to the onset of the permissive society, the upsurge of pornography and the casting aside of traditional sexual restraints. It surfaced in the Festival of Light in 1971 when thousands of slogan-shouting, sticker-bearing, placard-waving Christians marched around London and demonstrated for Jesus and against sin. It was a heady occasion when Christians realised that they were not a tiny, insignificant minority but could muster large crowds of highly motivated individuals with relative ease. We had power after all and were going on the offensive. We were the church militant. At the same time, I could not help feeling then that we were in danger of playing the world at its own game. We were flexing our muscles and taking to the streets in the same way we had seen others do of whom we disapproved.

The purpose of this chapter is to make the point that the language of battle is not without its dangers. This is of course true of any language that we apply to God. All our God-talk proceeds by analogy, using the language of the visible and known to describe the invisible and unknown. Of course it is only in the dynamic of God's self-revelation that we know which human words and concepts are appropriate and which are not. But there is a point at which every analogy becomes inadequate and breaks down. God and the spiritual world are too big to be comprehended by human language. We should bear this in mind in the use of battle language. There comes a point at which we can only use it if we also qualify it. If we do not correct the vocabulary of war and aggression with (for instance) that of peace and suffering love, we find ourselves spinning off onto a world of ungodly attitudes.

On the human level war is a cruel business and to wage it effectively people have got to become nasty. You cannot stick a bayonet into somebody in love. To do it you have to be filled with hate, fear, aggression and the adrenalin has to be flowing to make you do something that under normal conditions you never would. The experience of war indicates that once a war posture has been struck it is very difficult to control. The violence escalates. War cannot be strictly controlled or targeted against an exact aggressor. Innocent civilians get caught up in it, atrocities are committed by all sides. The engine of anger goes on running even when it is no longer needed. War brings every other evil in its train.

> Does not war demand that almost everything that God has forbidden be done on a broad front? To kill effectively, must not those who wage war steal, kill, rob, commit arson, lie, deceive, slander and unfortunately also to a large extent fornicate, not to speak of the almost inevitable repression of all the finer and weightier forms of obedience?[1]

Once Christians adopt the language, mentality and posture of spiritual war they are doing a necessary thing, but also a risky thing since they could so easily topple over into sin. The language of war is so blunt that they could lose their feeling for the finer qualities of justice, truth, mercy and gentleness and fail to see that Christian warfare is waged precisely through these qualities. When we speak of warfare therefore we need to revise radically the content and meaning of our speech. Spiritual warfare has its analogies to actual battle, but it is essentially and profoundly different. The Bible makes these distinctions and we will now set about tracing how this is done.

1. The identity of the enemy

Paul finds it necessary to stress that the enemies of God are not flesh and blood individuals but the invisible powers which stand behind them (Eph 6:12). He is here indicating that our enemies are not mere flesh and blood (and therefore weak) but strong and threatening. It must also mean that we are to resist the temptation to see people as our enemies. This is difficult to do because, invisible though the powers of darkness must be, they exert some of their agency through people, some of whom may adopt a threatening posture towards the church. It is difficult not to respond to such provocation in like manner. Yet our spiritual warfare is not assisted by adopting the methods of those who oppose us. Once we regard others as our enemies then the battle is half lost. It is *for* people that we wrestle with the invisible forces that enslave them and seek to enslave us. This is perfectly exemplified in the life of Jesus who drove out the prince of this world and yet treated his accusers, judges and crucifiers with compassion and respect.

Here we need to return to what we have described elsewhere as the 'paranoid worldview'. All of us, under pressure, will resort to paranoid attitudes. We will identify our enemies and blame them for our misfortune. So we will gain a degree of personal relief because we feel we have bottomed the situation. Paranoia pushes the blame on to another and enables us to feel relatively blameless. It is a psychological defence mechanism which helps us preserve an inner sense of being in the right. When spiritual warfare leads to our becoming paranoid about individuals, or groups of individuals we need to be wary. Paranoia and love cannot coexist. In naming the power of Islam, or witchcraft, or spiritualism as 'satanic', it becomes difficult to view those who are involved in these activities in any other way than as enemies. It erects a barrier between them and us which becomes difficult to cross, since fear and love do not easily dwell together. In denoting any of the structures of society as demonic we need to guard that we do not 'demonise' those who are involved in them. In the first chapter we referred to the witchcraft crazes of former generations, a horrible example of this tendency.

We should take care that we do not make even more blatant mistakes. Walter Wink makes a perceptive comment on this. He points out that in the interaction between good and evil there are four 'moments', or manifestations, which he indicates as follows:[2]

(1) God as God.
(2) God as 'Satan'.
(3) Satan as 'God'.
(4) Satan as Satan.

Moments (1) and (4) are relatively unproblematic. These are the times at which the activity of God or Satan is unambiguously seen for what it is. The complications come in moments (2) and (3) when the activity of God is perceived as that of Satan or that of Satan thought of as that of God.[3] According to Wink:

> A great deal that is creative or innovative is initially resisted as evil, and God's new creation is initially resisted as the work of the devil (God as 'Satan'). When Jesus turned aside the current messianic role as satanic, and began to act on the basis of just those words that were proceeding from the mouth of God, the authorities declared him an enemy of God. When he cast out demons and declared this to be a sign of the inbreaking kingdom, he was accused of being in cahoots with Beelzebub.[4]

So it is possible that what is truly of God is perceived as being Satanic because it appears as something new and threatening. God's will for justice, mercy and truth may be seen as evil by the powers that be with the consequence that Christians who are called to work for social transformation may even feel themselves to be stepping out beyond the pale when they do so. In this way it becomes possible to understand the way in which some Christians oppose godly social change because even they perceive it as something threatening and satanic, while others, who perceive the rightness of such change, have their moral nerve paralysed because they do not feel sure that what they think is God is not rationalised rebelliousness.[5]

To understand moment (3), Satan as 'God', we must see that Satan can masquerade as God. Paul says as much when he speaks of Satan masquerading as an angel of light (2 Cor 11:14). That which actually belongs to Satan's activity can look and feel as if it is God. Here we have the word of warning which is necessary when we begin to see others as enemies. It is the danger that we ourselves, in thinking that we are opposing Satan may fall prey to satanic attitudes and become as much in the wrong as that which we are resisting. This is what happens when Christians become rigidly legalistic, or morally slack. When we are hostile towards those who are different or project evil onto others whom we regard as 'demonic' and believe that we are doing God's will, we ourselves become satanic. It is possible to apply this 'Satan as God' concept to Christian attitudes to the homosexual community. Without wanting in any way to condone the practice of homosexuality, it needs to be said that the homophobia, the fear and hostility which some Christians manifest towards homosexuals, risks losing sight of them as people and demonising them. It is then the church which is at fault. Yet such attitudes masquerade as moral rectitude and concern for biblical values.

People are not our enemies and we should not treat them as such. To do so is to drive out the possibility of responding to them with the love and compassion of Jesus. The true enemies are the spiritual powers which are beyond people and we too are prone to adopt satanic attitudes. This is why Jesus rebuked Peter moments after he confessed him as Messiah (Mk 8:33). What is needed is that we see how Satan is equally willing to 'suit up for either team'.[6]

He is equally willing to stir up opposition to the church or to stir up wrong attitudes within it. Simplistic, black and white scenarios which see the church on one side as the faultless community and others as the corrupt enemy lead to the demonising of opponents and the failure to love our enemies. The history of the church proves the case. We need only refer to the Crusades to get the point. We need to recognise the shadow across our own lives and the nuances of satanic activity and to be self-critical.

2. The weapons we use

In spiritual warfare we also must qualify the nature of our weaponry. According to Paul, 'the weapons we fight with are not the weapons of the world' (2 Cor 10:4). The spiritual conflict needs to be fought on a spiritual level. It is not through physical or psychological weapons that the enemy is defeated. Once more the language of warfare needs to be qualified. It is not only that we should strike the right enemy; we must do so in the right way and with the right weapons.

Here we should dwell on the title of this particular chapter. The church faces a choice between the love of power and the power of love. Inevitably when the warfare image is deployed we begin to speak about power. War is conflict between different blocks of power. The church must beware that in the struggle for society we are not just struggling to maintain the powerful position that we have traditionally occupied in our society. Perhaps part of what has called forth a more militant Christianity in recent years is not concern for the kingdom of God but the fear that we are losing control and not getting our own way as we used to. But when we play the world at its own game of being hungry for power, for cultural dominance, have we not already lost the battle? Power corrupts. A symptom of its corruption is that we find ourselves using the world's weapons. When Christians, or their organisations, bend the truth, massage statistics, use sensational headlines, deal in rumours, despise their 'enemies', behave aggressively, use the levers of power to their own advantage, they are behaving no differently from the rest of society.

Christian faith and worldly power do not mix. When the attempt is made to fuse them the faith becomes corrupted. If we think that spiritual warfare is about the ability of Christians to dominate the institutional life of society and compel conformity to a supposedly Christian ethic we are mistaken. History plainly shows that, however well intentioned, the attempt by the church to back righteousness with coercive power distorts the gospel. This does not mean that there is no place for the enforcement of law. It does mean that the role of the church is to argue and persuade to produce a consensus that may then be translated into voluntarily accepted legislation, rather than to use the remnants of its past power to impose legislation upon a largely unwilling population. Such power as the church has must be 'influence with' rather than 'power over'.

When the church has become a coercive force attempting to impose its own version of the moral code it has strayed a long way from Christ. Historian Ramsey MacMullen has sought to describe how the early church grew within the Roman Empire and by what means it did so.[7] Within two centuries the church grew to be 'all but in a majority' in many cities in the Empire. From 100 AD it grew by half a million in every generation until by 312 AD there were five million Christians comprising one twelfth of the total population. In 313 AD the Edict of Milan promulgated by Emperor Constantine legalised the Christian religion and gave it official status. From 312 AD to 380 AD there followed what McMullen calls the 'Period of Flattery' when inducements were offered by the state for people to become Christians. This was followed by the 'Period of Battery' between 380 AD and 390 AD with the attempt to coerce people to enter the church. Church growth during these latter two periods was very rapid, yet the kind of Christianity it produced was corrupt, based as it was on flattery or battery.

The conclusion to be drawn is that the alliance of the church with the state which followed the Edict of Milan was probably the worst thing that happened to the church. It took it away from being a persecuted minority to being a persecuting majority. We are still seeking to recover from this disaster. We should see significance in the fact that the turning point came for the church in 312 AD when Constantine won the battle at the Milvian Bridge which led to his becoming emperor. Before the battle, Constantine had a vision which showed him what he must do to defeat his enemies. As told by Constantine to the historian Eusebius, as he was praying he had a vision of a cross of light in the heavens bearing the inscription 'Conquer by this'. He was commanded to make a likeness of it and to use it in his encounters with his enemies. The likeness was the Chi-Rho monogram which is still used as a Christian symbol.[8] What is significant is that Constantine was inspired by a distortion of the battle imagery which is part of Christian vocabulary. The battle was interpreted in physical terms in which the weapons are far from being spiritual. This is an example of the danger of using the language of battle wrongly and then exploiting it for the wrong ends.

If not by the exercise of worldly and coercive power, then by which weapons should spiritual warfare be waged? Here we must refer to Jesus as our example. He deliberately refused the temptation to worldly power and came neither as a military nor a political messiah. He came healing the sick, liberating the oppressed and identifying with the poor and outcast. He was both respectful and critical towards the political and religious authorities. The upshot was that he died in weakness upon a cross, sacrificing himself in love for his enemies and his friends. It is in this way that he destroyed the hold of the devil, soaked up evil by his atoning death and gained the victory over death as proclaimed and revealed in his resurrection. It was by the power of gracious and forgiving love that he disarmed the powers and principalities. He overcame evil by good. He resisted the temptation to overcome hostility by meeting it with an equal and opposite hostility, which is the automatic reaction of sinful human beings. Instead, he met it with steadfast and unflinching love in accordance with his own teaching on the Sermon on the Mount: 'Love your enemies and pray for those who persecute you, that you may be sons of your Father in heaven' (Mt 5:44). This is further illustrated by the problematic saying of Matthew 5:39: 'But I tell you, Do not resist an evil person.' As it stands, this verse seems difficult as it appears to enjoin a passive attitude towards wrongdoers allowing them to triumph. It could be held to prescribe a certain kind of response in the specific circumstances the chapter then goes on to describe, rather than an absolute position of non-resistance.[9] Alternatively the Greek text could contain an instrumental dative which would require a translation such as, 'Do not resist *by means of evil*'. What is here commanded is not carelessness or non-resistance on matters of principle but the response of love to individuals who may insult or misuse us.[10] This reflects the behaviour of Jesus who both denounced wrongdoing and behaved forgivingly to wrongdoers. Jesus shows how spiritual warfare is engaged in, not by hostility, aggression and the use of power but by the power of love. This must be how the church goes about its task. What exactly this might mean we attempt to set out in the last chapter.

3. The battle that is waged

A third area where the Bible qualifies the language of war concerns the battle that is waged, specifically as to whose battle it is. In the revival of military metaphors in the songs of the church the point has not always been clear that the battle belongs to the Lord. It is not helpful for us to sing about how we are going to destroy the enemy and execute justice because this obscures the fact that the battle is God's rather than ours and that the battle has already been won. What is needed is for us to concentrate upon the Lord as the warrior rather than ourselves. Indeed the theme of the helplessness of the people of God in the face of the enemy is deeply rooted in Scripture. It is not we who are a match for the enemy but the Lord and our eyes are upon him.[11] The drift of the Old Testament teaching is not that the people of God should become strong in order to overcome, but that they should remain vulnerable in order that they would need to trust in God in order to protect them. Basic to the Old Testament witness is that Yahweh fought by means of miracle, not through the armies of his people: 'it was not by your sword or your bow' (Josh 24:12). For this reason the primary agent in the holy war was not so much the warrior as the prophet who interpreted what God was doing.[12]

With this in mind it is striking that the kind of warfare envisaged in Ephesians 6:10–18 is defensive. The soldier of Christ is told to stand (vv11–14), to resist the onslaught of the devil, rather than to advance and take his territory. Here is a useful corrective. It is Christ who advances and Christians who are called to stand. This should caution Christians from having too exalted an idea of themselves in the conflict. We do not spearhead the advance of the kingdom. It is incorrect to talk of Christians 'bringing the kingdom'. The kingdom of God is like the mustard seed, or yeast (Mt 13:31–33) which mysteriously grows or ferments. The kingdom comes of itself. They may pray for its coming, may serve it and may even hasten it. But they cannot bring it. This is God's work. To have it otherwise puts too much emphasis on man, even militant Christian man, and not enough on God. It is not necessary for Christians to bind the strong man as if he had not already been bound. If Christ is now the head of every rule and authority and has driven out the prince of this world, then it is somewhat presumptuous for Christians to bind the 'spirits' of nations. They should rather pray for the nation and for the greater coming of the kingdom. It may be that along the way there are aspects of the work of the power of darkness which need to be confronted and frustrated by the word of authority in the name of Christ. But the assumption that guides our behaviour apart from these isolated moments is that Christ has bound the powers and is now making them a footstool for his feet. We should not try to fight a battle he has already won since this is to give unwarranted credibility to the defeated powers. We should rather pray that the kingdom may come in greater fullness. We live in the confident expectation of the revelation of Christ's victory and not in the frantic fear that unless we do something the powers will rampage unchecked. This attitude enables us to engage in the warfare that remains with a serene and strong faith in God's ultimate victory and not with a hagridden fear that it all depends on us.

A further cautionary word is appropriate. The kingdom of God will not come in its fullness until the Lord appears. It is then that the kingdoms of this world will become the kingdom of our God and of his Christ. Our task now is to prepare the way for that day. The role of Christians is not that of an occupying, invading army but of a subversive guerilla force. Perfection will elude us in the here and now. If we aim at a fully Christianised society we will be disappointed. We are to subvert and weaken as best we are able the power of an alienated world and the forces at work within it. We are looking forward and preparing for the day when God will take full possession of his world.

How should we go about this task? The final chapter will point the way ahead in some detailed ways. Overall, it must be by imitating Christ, by using the weapons of self-giving love and compassion, by identifying with the outcast and the poor rather than the rich and powerful and by refusing to continue the vicious cycle of human hostility and aggression.

REFERENCES

1. Karl Barth CD III/4 p454.
2. Wink *Unmasking the Powers* p35.
3. ibid.
4. ibid p35 cf Mk 3:22.
5. ibid.
6. ibid p33.
7. Ramsey MacMullen *Christianizing the Roman Empire* (New Haven and London, 1984).
8. K. S. Latourette *A History of the Expansion of Christianity. Volume I: The First Five Centuries* (Grand Rapids, 1970) p158.
9. David Hill *The Gospel of Matthew* (London, 1972) p128.
10. R. T. France *Matthew* (Leicester, 1985) p126.
11. Eg Ex 15:1–8; 2 Chron 20:21–6.
12. Millard C. Lind *Yahweh is a Warrior* (Scottdale 1980) p23.

CHAPTER TEN

What Kind of Church?

The church of Jesus Christ is the church militant. We are engaged in spiritual conflict and need to be equipped for this task. To be sure, the conflict is like no other form of battle. The weapons are quite different from any other weapons. We must rethink our notions of warfare. Yet the analogy is a valid one. Soldiers must be trained, disciplined, determined and fit if they are to fulfil their task. They must be equipped with the best weapons.

The apostle Paul was well acquainted with Roman soldiers. He spent a good part of his life being guarded by them. He may even at times have been chained to one. Out of his knowledge of a soldier's equipment he was able to write the description of spiritual armour that we have in Ephesians 6:13–18. Yet there is a significant difference between bodily and spiritual armour. The soldier's armour was something external that he put on and took off. The Christian's armour is what he or she actually is. It is their very being, the quality of the life that is lived. The Christian puts on the armour (Eph 6:13) in the same way that he or she 'puts on' or is 'clothed with' Christ (Rom 13:14; Gal 3:27). It is by being transformed by the Spirit into the likeness of Christ that we are 'clothed' with Christ. In the same way, by being inwardly changed we become the kind of people who are able to engage in spiritual conflict. It is when we are marked by righteousness, truth, readiness to witness, faith and the redeemed life, knowledge of the Word of God and prayer that we have become soldiers in the spiritual sense. It is certain that to be so changed, an act of will is required from us. We must decide that this is the way we will be. But the armour of God is not something external which we can put on or take off at will. It is our very being as Christians that is being spoken of here. What kind of church ought the militant church to be? How will it hasten the coming of the kingdom of God and the final defeat of the power of darkness? By way of summary of what has already been expressed in this book, the following points may help to bring things into focus.

1. A believing church

The church must know what it is to bear the shield of faith. It must believe in God, Father, Son and Spirit and take him with absolute seriousness. The God who is revealed in Christ and of whom Scripture speaks is the God who is the source of our life. He is not a being on the margins of our existence. He is our existence. The whole of life belongs to him and it is in this God that we find the integrating centre of life. To believe in God means to be fully persuaded in our minds that he is the one revealed in Christ, to be committed in our will and our affections to knowing and loving him and to be occupied in our imagination and thoughts with the vision of God.

We have argued, and argue here again, that to believe in God means that we radically disbelieve in the power of darkness. This does not mean that we think it is an illusion. We are mindful of its reality. But belief in God means that we reject the power of darkness. We refuse to be drawn to it or mastered by it. We treat it with scorn as that which has been mastered and overcome by the Living God in Christ. We refuse to give it attention or glory. We are not impressed by it but see it for the whipped cur that it is. God is the source of our life and we are nourished by contemplating his beauty and knowing his joy.

2. A thinking church

Perhaps no challenge is as important for charismatic churches than the challenge of teaching their people to think. In large measure charismatic renewal has been about the reclaiming of the subconscious. In reaction to an overintellectual, cerebral Christianity, it has stressed intuitive, immediate awareness of the Spirit of God. It has argued that there is a case for the suprarational in the Christian's experience and that this is well evidenced in the life of Jesus, the early church and the spirituality of God's people throughout the ages. This is a welcome corrective. It is a valid reclaiming of the breadth of experience for God. The danger is that we throw the baby out with the bathwater if we teach people to devalue the quality of analytical, reflective thought which will provide the counterpoint to mystical experience. Without this commitment to thinking as a basic Christian discipline we are liable to lapse into superstition and irrationality. The result will be that we will interpret wrongly our intuitive and mystical experiences and become prey to the dark power masquerading as an angel of light.

Theology is the church thinking through its faith. Charismatic Christians must give themselves to this task. Truth is part of our armour and the best way to counteract lies is to expose them with the truth. Enthusiasm and assertiveness are no substitute for clarity and persuasiveness of argument. If it is true that the devil is the father of lies (Jn 8:44), then speaking truth is part of the unmasking process. If it is true that Christians also are liable to be deceived (Lk 21:8) then we need for our own sakes to think carefully about the faith we profess in order that we may keep, and be kept, in the truth of Christ. In the history of the church, it is clear that when Christians have been able to articulate their faith clearly and persuasively truth has tended to prevail over the lie.

3. A proclaiming church

The Word of God is part of Christian weaponry. When the Word of God is preached in the power of the Spirit there is a spiritual power at work which is potent. The reason is clear enough. When it is preached God himself is present in his Word. The events of cross and resurrection become contemporary realities. From this a number of conclusions must be drawn.

Firstly: It is a mistake to think of spiritual warfare as a kind of esoteric, elitist activity which super-Christians engage in and which is a million miles away from what ordinarily happens when the church gathers. The reverse is the case. It is in the 'ordinary' activities of the Christian community that spiritual warfare has its heart. As the Word of God is preached and expounded week by week, spiritual warfare is engaged in and a boundary is set across which the power of darkness may not go. The power which rules through lies and deception is shown up to be what it is through the message of Christ crucified.

Secondly: for this to be the case, it must be the Word of God which is preached. The opinions of men are not spiritually potent. Anecdotes and experiences may have their value in illustrating the preached word, but they are not of themselves the Word of God. The renewing work of the Spirit of God is exercised through and by the exposition of the meaning of Scripture. Therefore the proclaiming church must give attention to its own preaching in order that it may truly be the Word of God.

Thirdly: the proclaiming church is misunderstood if the image which comes to mind is purely that of pulpits and pews. The Word of God must be expounded in the church, it is true. But preaching is far more than this. To train preachers to be good pulpit performers can be very misleading and incestuous if they are not also taught to engage the world in their proclamation. In the New Testament pulpits did not exist. The vast majority of sermons there recorded were not preached in the church but in the world. Preaching is not pulpiteering. It is the total activity of the church in its verbal communication of the gospel.

4. A praying church

As with preaching, praying is part of the very essence of the church and is itself, wherever and whenever it is found, part of our spiritual warfare. Paul tells the church at Ephesus to 'pray in the Spirit on all occasions with all kinds of prayers and requests' (Eph 6:18). Recently the custom has developed in the church of praying 'against' things. Whatever the justification of this may be, and it is not well represented in the New Testament, our first responsibility is to pray *for* the world. This means putting ourselves in the role of the sympathetic participant in the drama of human affairs and on the basis of the love of God for all praying for the community, nation and world.

When we pray something happens in the invisible realm which undergirds and affects the visible realm. We should confess straightaway that prayer is a mystery. It can only be understood if we presuppose that human history does not have the nature of a predetermined outworking of fate but of an interactive dialogue between God and humanity.

191

In this interaction the process of history is formed and the world moves towards its ultimate goal. When Christians pray, they engage in the divine–human interaction and are involved with God on behalf of the human family in the coming of His kingdom. In prayer it is as if God is given access into human affairs. When the Word became flesh he came into a circle of devout, praying individuals and families (Mt 1:18–25; Lk 1:6). In the same way through the prayers of his people, the God who holds all things together gains greater access to the life of estranged humanity. It is very much the case therefore that the prayers of God's people will serve the activity of the Holy Spirit in the world and will act as a boundary to that of evil. No doubt this is why Jesus taught his disciples to pray, 'Your kingdom come, your will be done, on earth as it is in heaven.'

5. A loving church

We have gone to some pains to argue that at this point in particular spiritual warfare must be carefully understood. War is not naturally identifiable with love. The danger is that those who take the warfare seriously adopt aggressive and militant attitudes which drive out the loving-kindness that we see in Jesus. How can Christians, for instance, resist the practice of homosexuality without at the same time alienating homosexuals and projecting an attitude of rejection towards them? We must face the fact that what we feel to be righteous indignation can communicate itself as persecution. Frequently, the church finds itself on the horns of a dilemma here. The demands of moral theology make the church want to condemn sin. The demands of pastoral theology make the church want to love sinners. When the church condemns sin, she is accused of not caring for sinners. When she cares for sinners she is accused of being soft on sin!

How do we get it right? Jesus had a striking ability to combine a clear call for righteousness with a great love for sinners. This is seen most clearly in the narrative of the woman taken in adultery (Jn 8:1–11). The Pharisees are clearly using the woman's situation to trap Jesus and he appears to be faced with the choice either of joining in their censorious and judgemental attitudes or of rejecting the teaching of the Old Testament on adultery. In the event he neither allows himself to be drawn into their attitudes, thereby treating the woman as a non-person, nor into condoning her sin. By treating the woman as a person and showing compassion to her, he gives her every incentive to leave behind her sin.

When Christians in the name of morality give way to moralistic and judgemental attitudes which lose sight of individuals they run the risk of being like the Pharisees whom Jesus so clearly distanced himself from. We do well to imitate Jesus in projecting a love for individuals which accepts them as they are and refuses to strike a condemnatory pose, while at the same time being shot through with a strong and pure morality which is in no doubt that the wellbeing of each individual lies along the pathway of moral living. When it came to dealing with the powerless and victimised Jesus demonstrated this attitude consistently. When it came to the powerful he showed himself to be strong and forthright in condemnation.

6. A discerning church

There is more to the gift of discernment than suspicion. The latter quality is regrettably in far greater supply than the former. We are all good at concocting conspiracy theories and the Christian's attitude to the demonic can be wrongly determined by this. Because something happens that does not quite fit our plan it does not necessarily mean that there is demonic interference. Frequently people excuse themselves from failure in relationships by saying euphemistically 'the enemy got in'. There are those who tenaciously refuse to accept the truth about their own weaknesses of character or behaviour by construing criticism as satanic attack. Such language uses the devil as a convenient dustbin in which to dump their own garbage. He is a cypher for externalising failure and sin. By projecting sin onto the external screen of the devil, responsibility is avoided.

My point is that this is not discernment. It is symbolic speech that betrays a mental attitude. There is too much of it around. It functions as a 'sorting myth' whereby we feel we have bottomed a situation by reference to a basic motif. Actually we may be deceiving ourselves. There are times when the devil should be left out of things since the truth of a situation is obscured and not clarified by resort to such a thought. A discerning church does not 'think devil'. It ignores the devil most of the time and perceives him at work only where he actually is. Just as we need extreme care before denoting a pastoral situation 'demonic' so in the life of church and community such a diagnosis should only be put forward where it is genuinely appropriate. Otherwise we get the devil a bad name. The church should be healthily sceptical of pseudo-spiritual language and yet truly discerning, attuned by the Spirit of God and the Word of God to discern the spirits.

7. An authoritative church

What do we do when we discern the work of the devil in a given situation? We are not left defenceless. The church does not have in its armoury the kind of coercive power that the world uses. Yet she is powerful with a power that is fundamentally different in that it is not a power over people to oppress or control them, but a power over the forces of evil to banish and frustrate them. This power sets people free. It is rooted in the authority of Jesus of whom it is recorded, 'he drove out the spirits with a word' (Mt 8:16) and 'with authority and power he gives orders to evil spirits and they come out' (Lk 4:36).

Authority is vested in believers when they speak and operate in the name and by the Spirit of Jesus. This authority does not function outside of Christ and is essentially his authority mediated from time to time through the believer and the believing community. So Jesus speaks to his disciples and says, 'I have given you authority to trample on snakes and scorpions and to overcome all the power of the enemy' (Lk 10:19). Through the word of the believer the power of the enemy is overcome. When the believer, having discerned enemy activity, speaks in the name of Jesus to overcome it, it is the presence and authority of Christ in that action and word which is the effective agent. This is not a magical power which functions at the believer's discretion but the authority of Christ active in the believer. This is where the gift of discernment is crucial. To use authoritative words undiscerningly runs the risk of treating the power of God as if it were something to be conjured up at will. To use such language as a matter of routine rather than one of discernment borders on the magic mentality. For instance, occasionally it is possible to hear someone binding the devil in prayer so that a meeting will go well. This is not because there has been a moment of discernment but because it is presumed that the devil must be at work unless we bind him. Authority is being used here as a fetish. If we need the reassurance that God is in control, why not simply affirm this fact and thank him for it?

195

8. A listening church

A concern which has emerged in this book is that we do not use the language of spiritual battle to produce or to excuse wrong attitudes towards those whom we might consider enemies. This has been described as the paranoid mentality. Not infrequently, wrong behaviour is justified in spiritual terms. In failing to consult people or to behave courteously it is sometimes considered sufficient excuse that 'the Lord told me to do it'. The sense of spiritual conviction however should never be seen as a substitute for decent behaviour. It creates a cynicism about spiritual things. It brings disrepute upon the fact that there are times when God *does* tell us to do things. The fact that we are engaged in spiritual warfare does not excuse us from seeking to listen to what others are saying, even those with whom we may disagree. It is only when we listen with respect, sincerity and love that we can really perceive what the spiritual issues are and where the battlefield really lies.

Wise words were spoken in this area by the Jewish philosopher Martin Buber (1878–1965). He argued that mankind knows two kinds of attitudes. There is the I–It attitude which marks our attitude to the inanimate world. We relate to it as a thing and know it as such. The other is the I–Thou attitude in which God and our fellows are made known to us in personal relationships. We cannot know God or others through an I–It attitude. Buber goes on to say that in what Christians would call evangelism we need to develop I–Thou relationships of love and appreciative understanding of others, not the I–It approach which seeks to make proselytes by confrontation and loses sight of the fact that we are dealing with persons.[1]

This is relevant to the militant church. In being militant it is necessary to stress that we are called to be lovingly militant and to achieve that same remarkable blend of discerning and authoritative opposition to evil combined with gracious and accepting openness to people that we see in the life of Jesus. We cannot truly love people without taking time to understand them and their ideas. To engage in dialogue with others whether Marxist, humanist, Moslem or pagan, ardent feminist or homosexual does not mean that we lessen our own convictions but that we accept others as made in the image of God.

9. A free church

The final quality which we mention is that we be a free people. We cannot co-operate with God in freeing the world of the power of darkness unless we ourselves know that freedom. To be sure, final and complete freedom awaits the consummation. We will struggle with the darkness until the day when Christ brings the whole creation into its ultimate liberty. Personal temptations and sometimes failure will accompany the life of God's people until the coming of the Lord. There is no room therefore for the spirit of self-confident triumphalism. We are not free of the shadow. But into today there has come the liberating power of tomorrow which affords a foretaste of a glorious future. We have been set free from the power of the evil one to serve the Living God. This is manifested in the freedom we have to worship and serve God, laying aside the old works of darkness in favour of pure and holy living.

If the spiritual authority of the church is lacking it is linked with the unwillingness of those who have been set free to live in freedom. While imprisoned by futile sins, uncaring, bigoted and unChristian attitudes, and by conformist, worldly behaviour we lessen our effectiveness for God. It is truly free people who will serve God's purpose of liberation most effectively. Such living is what the devil now seeks to thwart. There is a battlefield in our hearts and in the church. This battle needs to be won for the sake of the wider battle in the world. Yet even here, a strategy of darkness is to discourage us. When we see failure in the church we are tempted to despair. Even this discouragement must be refused as we confess that the church belongs to Jesus Christ and he is working his purpose out.

The signs of Christ's victory are all around us. They are to be seen in the conversions that take place daily, in the healing of lives and homes, in the faithful and sacrificial service of millions of Christians, in the renewing of old churches and the planting of new ones, the growth of trust and confidence, the thoughtful engagement with the world. There are indeed setbacks and failures but Christ is building his church and the gates of hell will not prevail against it. Already the power of darkness has been put in its place. Those who know this should bear it in mind. The time will soon dawn when Christ's victory will be finally revealed and the power of darkness will have had its day.

He who testifies to these things says, 'Yes, I am coming soon'. Amen. Come, Lord Jesus (Rev 22:30).

REFERENCE

1. Martin Buber *I and Thou* (Edinburgh, 1937); *Between Man and Man* (London and Glasgow, 1962) pp17–36.